004.1675
M896k5

DETROIT PUBLIC LIBRARY

☞ **W9-BLZ-204**

Kindle Fire™
HDX

FOR

DUMMIES®

A Wiley Brand

CHASE BRANCH LIBRARY
17731 W. SEVEN MILE RD.
DETROIT, MI 48235
578-8002

MAR -- 2015
CH

CHASE BRANCH LIBRARY
17731 W. SEVEN MILE RD.
DETROIT, MI 48235
578-8002

Kindle Fire™ HDX

FOR DUMMIES®

A Wiley Brand

by Nancy Muir

FOR DUMMIES®

A Wiley Brand

Kindle Fire™ HDX For Dummies®

Published by: **John Wiley & Sons, Inc.,** 111 River Street, Hoboken, NJ 07030-5774, www.wiley.com

Copyright © 2014 by John Wiley & Sons, Inc., Hoboken, New Jersey

Media and software compilation copyright © 2014 by John Wiley & Sons, Inc. All rights reserved.

Published simultaneously in Canada

No part of this publication may be reproduced, stored in a retrieval system or transmitted in any form or by any means, electronic, mechanical, photocopying, recording, scanning or otherwise, except as permitted under Sections 107 or 108 of the 1976 United States Copyright Act, without the prior written permission of the Publisher. Requests to the Publisher for permission should be addressed to the Permissions Department, John Wiley & Sons, Inc., 111 River Street, Hoboken, NJ 07030, (201) 748-6011, fax (201) 748-6008, or online at http://www.wiley.com/go/permissions.

Trademarks: Wiley, For Dummies, the Dummies Man logo, Dummies.com, Making Everything Easier, and related trade dress are trademarks or registered trademarks of John Wiley & Sons, Inc. and may not be used without written permission. Kindle Fire is a trademark of Amazon Technologies, Inc. All other trademarks are the property of their respective owners. John Wiley & Sons, Inc. is not associated with any product or vendor mentioned in this book.

LIMIT OF LIABILITY/DISCLAIMER OF WARRANTY: THE PUBLISHER AND THE AUTHOR MAKE NO REPRESENTATIONS OR WARRANTIES WITH RESPECT TO THE ACCURACY OR COMPLETENESS OF THE CONTENTS OF THIS WORK AND SPECIFICALLY DISCLAIM ALL WARRANTIES, INCLUDING WITHOUT LIMITATION WARRANTIES OF FITNESS FOR A PARTICULAR PURPOSE. NO WARRANTY MAY BE CREATED OR EXTENDED BY SALES OR PROMOTIONAL MATERIALS. THE ADVICE AND STRATEGIES CONTAINED HEREIN MAY NOT BE SUITABLE FOR EVERY SITUATION. THIS WORK IS SOLD WITH THE UNDERSTANDING THAT THE PUBLISHER IS NOT ENGAGED IN RENDERING LEGAL, ACCOUNTING, OR OTHER PROFESSIONAL SERVICES. IF PROFESSIONAL ASSISTANCE IS REQUIRED, THE SERVICES OF A COMPETENT PROFESSIONAL PERSON SHOULD BE SOUGHT. NEITHER THE PUBLISHER NOR THE AUTHOR SHALL BE LIABLE FOR DAMAGES ARISING HEREFROM. THE FACT THAT AN ORGANIZATION OR WEBSITE IS REFERRED TO IN THIS WORK AS A CITATION AND/OR A POTENTIAL SOURCE OF FURTHER INFORMATION DOES NOT MEAN THAT THE AUTHOR OR THE PUBLISHER ENDORSES THE INFORMATION THE ORGANIZATION OR WEBSITE MAY PROVIDE OR RECOMMENDATIONS IT MAY MAKE. FURTHER, READERS SHOULD BE AWARE THAT INTERNET WEBSITES LISTED IN THIS WORK MAY HAVE CHANGED OR DISAPPEARED BETWEEN WHEN THIS WORK WAS WRITTEN AND WHEN IT IS READ.

For general information on our other products and services, please contact our Customer Care Department within the U.S. at 877-762-2974, outside the U.S. at 317-572-3993, or fax 317-572-4002. For technical support, please visit www.wiley.com/techsupport.

Wiley publishes in a variety of print and electronic formats and by print-on-demand. Some material included with standard print versions of this book may not be included in e-books or in print-on-demand. If this book refers to media such as a CD or DVD that is not included in the version you purchased, you may download this material at http://booksupport.wiley.com. For more information about Wiley products, visit www.wiley.com.

Library of Congress Control Number: 2013949561

ISBN: 978-1-118-77265-2

ISBN 978-1-118-77265-2 (pbk); ISBN 978-1-118-77266-9 (ebk); ISBN 978-1-118-77580-6 (ebk)

Manufactured in the United States of America

10 9 8 7 6 5 4 3 2 1

Contents at a Glance

Introduction 1

Part I: Getting Started with Kindle Fire HDX 5
Chapter 1: Overview of the Kindle Fire HDX 7
Chapter 2: Kindle Fire HDX Quickstart 23
Chapter 3: Kindle Fire HDX Settings 49

Part II: Taking the Leap Online 75
Chapter 4: Going Shopping 77
Chapter 5: Going Online 99

Part III: Having Fun and Getting Productive 123
Chapter 6: E-Reader Extraordinaire... 125
Chapter 7: Playing Music 151
Chapter 8: Playing Video... 167
Chapter 9: Going Social 181
Chapter 10: Getting Productive with Kindle Fire HDX 197

Part 4: The Part of Tens 223
Chapter 11: Ten Apps That Add Functionality to Kindle Fire HDX 225
Chapter 12: Ten (or So) Top Gaming Apps 239

Index 253

Table of Contents

Introduction *1*

About This Book 1
Foolish Assumptions 2
Icons Used in This Book 2
Beyond the Book 3
Where to Go from Here 3

Part I: Getting Started with Kindle Fire HDX *5*

Chapter 1: Overview of the Kindle Fire HDX 7

What's New in Kindle Fire HDX 7
A Quick Rundown of Kindle Fire HDX
   Hardware Features 9
Key Features of Kindle Fire HDX 10
   Storage on Earth and in the Cloud 10
   App appeal 11
   Pre-installed functionality 12
   The magic of Whispersync 14
   You want content — Amazon's got it 15
   Browsing with Amazon Silk 17
   A world of color on the display 19
   Understanding the value of Amazon Prime 19

Chapter 2: Kindle Fire HDX Quickstart 23

Get Going with Kindle Fire HDX 23
Getting to Know the Interface 32
   Accessing Kindle Fire HDX libraries 34
   Playing with the Carousel 38
   Getting on the grid 38
   Getting clues from the Status bar 41
   The often-present, ever-changing Options bar 44
   The Navigation panel 46
Using a Micro USB Cable to Transfer Data 46

Chapter 3: Kindle Fire HDX Settings 49

Opening Quick Settings 49
   Controlling spin with Auto-Rotate 50
   Turning up the Brightness 51

Flying high with Airplane Mode 52
Relaxing with Quiet Time.. 53
Sending out a Mayday 53
Finding Other Settings 54
Sync All Content.. 55
My Account.. 55
Help... 57
Parental Controls 58
Looking at device settings 61
Setting up Wireless and Networks.. 66
Working with applications.. 67
Choosing Settings for Notifications and Quiet Time 69
Controlling display and sounds 69
Working with the onscreen keyboard.. 71
New and Improved Accessibility Features 71
Making security settings 73

Part II: Taking the Leap Online 75

Chapter 4: Going Shopping 77

Managing Your Amazon Account 77
Visiting the Amazon Appstore 80
Exploring the world of apps 80
Searching for apps 81
Buying apps 83
Buying Content 86
Buying publications through Newsstand... 87
Buying books 90
Buying music 92
Buying video 95
Shopping for Anything Else.. 97

Chapter 5: Going Online 99

Getting Online by Using Wi-Fi 99
Browsing the Internet with Silk... 101
Using navigation tools to get around 101
Displaying tabs.. 102
Turning on Reading View 103
Bookmarking sites 103
Using Web content shortcuts.. 104
Choosing Silk's General settings 106
Searching for content on a page 108
Searching the web... 109
Reviewing browsing history 111
Working with web page content 113

Choosing Privacy Settings 114
Working with E-Mail 116
 Setting up an e-mail account 116
 Sending e-mail 117
 Receiving e-mail 119
 Forwarding and replying to e-mail 119
Sending E-Mail to Your Kindle Account 121

Part III: Having Fun and Getting Productive 123

Chapter 6: E-Reader Extraordinaire 125
So Many Things to Read! 126
 Buying books 126
 Using the Amazon Lending Library 127
 Borrowing from your local library 129
Reading Books 129
 Going to the (Books) library 130
 Opening a book 132
 Navigating a book 133
Diving In with Immersion Reading 135
X-Ray for Books 137
 Searching in a book 138
 Bookmarking a page and highlighting text 141
 Modifying the appearance of a page 143
 Sharing with others through Facebook or Twitter 145
Managing Publications 145
Buying and Reading Periodicals 148
Reading Docs on Kindle Fire HDX 150

Chapter 7: Playing Music 151
Exploring the Music Library 152
Searching for Music 154
Uploading Music to the Cloud 155
Playing Music 158
 Opening and playing a song 158
 X-Ray for Music 159
 Creating playlists 162
 Editing a playlist 165

Chapter 8: Playing Video 167
Streaming versus Downloading 167
Looking at Your Videos Library 170
 Navigating categories 170
 Creating Your Watchlist 172

Searching for and filtering content 172
Setting video quality...173
Opening and Playing a Video 173
Using Second Screen to Fling a Movie to Your TV 177
Using X-Ray for Video and Music 178

Chapter 9: Going Social..181

Managing Contacts 181
Importing contacts 182
Creating new contacts...183
Viewing and organizing contacts...186
Using Integrated Facebook and Twitter 189
Making Calls with Skype 191

Chapter 10: Getting Productive with Kindle Fire HDX.............197

Understanding Kindle Docs...198
Getting Docs onto Kindle Fire HDX 199
Grabbing docs from your computer..199
Sending docs by e-mail..200
Syncing with the Cloud 200
Understanding Document File Formats 202
Working with Docs...203
Opening docs..203
E-mailing docs 205
Printing docs: Coming soon..207
Working with OfficeSuite Pro 209
Opening a document in OfficeSuite Pro 209
Using editing tools 209
Staying on Time with Calendar 211
Calendar views 212
Syncing with a calendar account 213
Adding a new event 213
Taking and Viewing Photos and Video 213
Taking photos...214
Recording video 216
Getting photos onto Kindle Fire HDX..216
Viewing photos...216
Editing photos 218
Managing photos in the Amazon Cloud Drive................................221
Using the Oxford Dictionary of English 221

Part 4: The Part of Tens *223*

Chapter 11: Ten Apps That Add Functionality to Kindle Fire HDX...225

SketchBook Mobile...226
Calorie Counter and Diet Tracker 227
Alarm Clock Xtreme Free..228
Astral Budget...228
ColorNote Notepad Notes 230
Calculator Plus Free 230
AccuWeather..231
Bloomberg (Kindle Tablet Edition) 233
Convertr..235
Wifi Analyzer 236

Chapter 12: Ten (or So) Top Gaming Apps 239

Contre Jour..239
Monsters Ate My Condo 240
Where's My Perry? 242
Quell Memento...243
Blood and Glory: Legend 244
Stray Souls: Dollhouse Story 245
Chess Free 246
Bejeweled 2...247
Wordsmith...248
Solitaire Free Pack...249
Asphalt 8: Airborne 250
Words with Friends Free 251

Index *253*

Introduction

Kindle Fire HDX is a very affordable way to get at all kinds of media, from music and videos to books and colorful magazines. It's also a device that allows you to browse the Internet, connect to your Facebook account, make video calls via Skype, take photos, check your e-mail, and read documents. The portability of both the 7-inch and 8.9-inch models makes it incredibly useful for people on the go in today's fast-paced world.

In this book, I introduce you to all the cool features of Kindle Fire HDX, providing tips and advice for getting the most out of this ingenious little tablet. I help you find your way around its attractive and easy-to-use interface, provide advice about getting the most out of the Amazon Cloud Drive for storing content, and even recommend some neat apps that make your Kindle Fire HDX more functional and fun.

About This Book

"If Kindle Fire HDX is so easy to use, why do I need a book?" you may be asking yourself. When I first sat down with Kindle Fire HDX, it took about a week of poking around to find settings, features, and ways to buy and locate my content and apps. When was the last time you had a week to spare? I've spent the time so that you can quickly and easily get the hang of all the Kindle Fire HDX features and discover a few tricks I bet your friends won't uncover for quite a while.

This book uses certain conventions that are helpful to understand, including

- ✓ Text that you're meant to type just as it appears in the book is **bold**. The exception is when you're working through a step list: Because each step is bold, the text to type is not bold.

- ✓ Web addresses appear in `monofont`. If you're reading a digital version of this book on a device connected to the Internet, note that you can click the web address to visit that website, like this: `www.dummies.com`.

 This book covers many of the features in the original Kindle Fire, released in 2011, and the Kindle Fire HD, released in 2012, as well as the features that are new with the Kindle Fire HDX. Though this book is focused on Kindle Fire HDX, whichever Kindle Fire model you own, you should find lots of advice and answers in this book.

Foolish Assumptions

You may have opted for a tablet to watch movies and read books on the run. You might think it's a good way to browse business documents and check e-mail on your next plane trip. You might have one or more computers and be very computer savvy, or you might hate computers and figure that Kindle Fire HDX gives you all the computing power you need to browse the Internet and read e-books.

Kindle Fire HDX users come in all types. I don't assume in this book that you're a computer whiz, but I do assume that you have a passing understanding of how to copy a file and plug in a USB cable. I'm guessing you've browsed the Internet at least a few times and heard of Wi-Fi, which is what you use to go online with a Kindle Fire HDX (unless you purchase the LTE version). Other than that, you don't need a lot of technical background to get the most out of this book.

Icons Used in This Book

Icons are little pictures in the margin of this book that alert you to special types of advice or information, including

✏ These short words of advice draw your attention to faster, easier, or alternative ways of getting things done with Kindle Fire HDX.

✏ When you see this icon, you'll know that I'm emphasizing important information for you to keep in mind as you use a feature.

✏ There aren't too many ways you can get in trouble with the Kindle Fire HDX, but in those few situations where some action might be irreversible, I include warnings so you can avoid any pitfalls.

✏ If you're using a Kindle Fire HD, this icon will point out what features you might not have. If you've upgraded to HDX, you also get a clue as to cool new features to check out.

Beyond the Book

There is extra online content about Kindle Fire HDX that goes beyond the book itself. Go online to take advantage of these features:

- ✓ **Cheat Sheet** (www.dummies.com/cheatsheet/kindlefirehdx): The Cheat Sheet for this book includes a table of information about all the Quick Settings available to you, including settings to adjust screen brightness and the new MayDay online support button.

- ✓ **Dummies.com online articles:** The parts pages of this book provide links to articles on Dummies.com that extend the content covered in the book. The articles appear on the book's Extras page at www.dummies.com/extras/kindlefirehdx. Topics include Staying Safe Online, Getting More Out of OfficeSuite, and Ten Great Apps for Kids.

- ✓ **Updates:** Here's where you can find updates in case the book changes substantially www.dummies.com/extras/kindlefirehdx.

Where to Go from Here

Time to get that Kindle Fire HDX out of its box, set it up, and get going with all the fun, entertaining things it makes available to you. Have fun!

Part I
Getting Started with Kindle Fire HDX

 Visit www.dummies.com for more great content online.

In this part...

✔ Get your first glimpse at Kindle Fire HDX as it comes out of the box.

✔ Discover how to use the touchscreen and work with the Kindle Fire HDX interface.

✔ Step through useful Kindle Fire HDX settings to work with everything from connecting to a network to setting up the language your Kindle Fire uses.

Overview of the Kindle Fire HDX

In This Chapter

▶ Comparing Kindle Fire HDX to the competition

▶ Surveying all of the Kindle Fire HDX's features

*L*et's start at the beginning. A *tablet* is a handheld computer with a touchscreen and an onscreen keyboard for providing input, and with apps that allow you to play games, read e-books, check e-mail, browse the web, watch movies, listen to music, and more.

Amazon, the giant online retailer, just happens to have access to more content (music, movies, audio books, and so on) than just about anybody on the planet. So, when an Amazon tablet debuted a couple of years ago, and as Amazon stacked up media partnerships with the likes of Fox and PBS, the Kindle Fire tablet was seen as the first real challenge to Apple's iPad.

Now, in its third generation, the Kindle Fire HDX offers several very nice improvements at the right price and feature mix for many people, while offering the key to that treasure chest of content that Amazon has been wise enough to amass.

In this chapter, you get an overview of the Kindle Fire HDX: how it compares to competing devices and what its key features are. Subsequent chapters delve into how to use all those features in detail.

What's New in Kindle Fire HDX

Kindle Fire HDX and the new operating system, Fire OS 3.0, bring several new or improved features to the table, including:

✔ **Mayday:** A support feature that allows you to interact with a live tech advisor who can talk you through procedures, point out items on your screen by circling them, or actually take over your Kindle Fire and perform procedures for you.

✔ **X-Ray:** This feature was available on Kindle Fire HDs, but with Fire OS 3.0 it has been enhanced to provide information about books and music in addition to TV shows and movies. X-Ray makes available information about topics such as movie cast members and vocal artists, and can even display song lyrics as music plays.

✔ **Grid View:** The Favorites area in the lower part of the Home screen has been redesigned into a grid, the first two lines of which contain icons for commonly used apps such as the Silk browser and Email. You can add apps and content such as books and music selections to this grid so that you can access them more quickly.

✔ **Quiet Time:** If you don't want to hear notifications for events such as arriving mail or download completions for a time, just tap the Quiet Time button in the Quick Settings bar (swipe down from the top of the screen to display Quick Settings).

✔ **Quick Switch:** To see content and apps you've used recently, from any screen but the Home screen swipe up or to the left from the Options bar (depending on whether it's positioned at the bottom or on the right of the screen) to see a scrollable list. This Quick Switch feature lets you quickly jump to another option without returning to the Home screen.

✔ **Printing Support:** You can now print docs, photos, and e-mail messages to wireless printers.

✔ **Accessibility Tools:** Screen Reader, Explore by Touch, and Screen Magnifier have been added to help people with hearing or vision challenges. See Chapter 3 for more details about these features.

✔ **Second Screen:** This feature wasn't yet available when Kindle Fire HDX first shipped, but it will appear soon. It allows you to "fling" content on your Kindle Fire HDX or the Amazon Cloud to your television. This causes the content to stream to the TV so that your Kindle Fire HDX is freed up for you to do other things with it while watching.

✔ **Kindle FreeTime:** This improved feature lets you create a unique environment for your kids by limiting what content and apps they can use. When you turn on FreeTime, your kids see only the content you've given them permission to use, and it's all shown against a more kid-friendly graphical background.

✔ **Goodreads:** This service is like a social network for readers. You can download the free app and then track and share what you're reading and get access to reviews and recommendations from other readers.

✔ **Immersion Reading:** You can synchronize a book on your Kindle Fire HDX with an Audible audiobook. When you do, text in the e-book will be highlighted as each word is read from within the Kindle reader, which Amazon considers a more "immersive" reading experience to aid learning.

✔ **Kindle Matchbook:** This sales feature, coming out soon, allows you to get a discounted Kindle version of any book you've purchased on Amazon.

✔ **1-Tap-Archive:** If you haven't used an app in quite some time, say, a month or more, a check mark appears on it to indicate that it's not being used. If you want to remove the app from your Kindle Fire HDX, you can simply tap the app to do so.

A Quick Rundown of Kindle Fire HDX Hardware Features

Kindle Fire HDX comes in two sizes: 7 inches (see Figure 1-1) and 8.9 inches. Improvements with the third generation HDX include a faster processor, longer battery life, and higher screen resolution in both models. The 8.9-inch model includes both front- and rear-facing cameras, and both models offer dual microphones.

Figure 1-1: The neat size and weight of Kindle Fire HDX make it easy to hold.

Looking for your Kindle Fire HDX speaker? With this latest model, it has been moved from the back of the device to the top.

Table 1-1 provides an at-a-glance view of Kindle Fire HDX features.

Table 1-1	Kindle Fire HDX Specifications
Feature	*Kindle Fire HDX Specs*
Display size	7 inches or 8.9 inches
Processor	2.2 GHz quad-core Snapdragon 800 processor
Screen resolution	1920 × 1200 on 7 inch; 2560 × 1600 on 8.9 inch

(continued)

Table 1-1 *(continued)*

Feature	Kindle Fire HDX Specs
Internal storage	16GB, 32GB, or 64GB
Battery life	11 hours, or 17 hours for reading only
Price	7-inch model is $229 for 16GB and $269 for 32GB, and $309 for 64GB; 8.9-inch model is $379 for 16GB, $429 for 32GB, and $479 for 64GB
Content	Amazon Appstore
Connectivity	Wi-Fi or 4G LTE
Ports	Micro USB to connect to your computer
Browser	Silk
Camera	Front-facing HDX for 7 inch and 8.9 inch; rear-facing 8 MP for 8.9 inch only
Sound	3.5 mm stereo jack; dual stereo speakers, Dolby Digital Plus sound
Volume control	Physical volume rocker switch

Key Features of Kindle Fire HDX

Kindle Fire HDX is a tablet device with all the things most people want from a tablet packed into an easy-to-hold package: e-mail, web browsing, players for video and music content, built-in calendar and contacts apps, an e-reader, a great online content store, access to tens of thousands of Android apps, and so on. In the following sections, you get to explore all these useful features.

Storage on Earth and in the Cloud

Kindle Fire HDX offers 16GB, 32GB, or 64GB of storage in its 7- and 8.9-inch models. Any storage amount will probably work just fine for you because when you own a Kindle Fire HDX, you get free, unlimited Amazon Cloud Drive storage for all digital content purchased from Amazon (but not content that you copy onto Kindle Fire HDX from your computer by connecting a micro USB cable). This means that books, movies, music, and apps are held online for you to stream or download at any time you have access to Wi-Fi, instead of being stored on your Kindle Fire HDX.

This Amazon Cloud Drive storage means that you don't use up your Kindle Fire HDX memory. As long as you have a Wi-Fi connection, you can stream content from Amazon Cloud at any time. If you'll be away from a connection, download an item (such as an episode of your favorite TV show), watch it, and then remove it from your device the next time you're within range of a Wi-Fi network. The content is still available in the Cloud: You can download that content again or stream it anytime you like.

If you want to go whole hog into Kindle Fire HDX, you can opt for the highest memory device, the 64GB 8.9-inch Kindle Fire HDX 4G LTE Wireless version of the device. Just be aware that 4G devices come with the added cost of an AT&T or Verizon data plan.

App appeal

Kindle Fire HDX is generally easy to use, with a simple, Android-based touch-screen interface. Its primary focus is on consuming media — and consuming media is what Amazon is all about. Kindle Fire HDX also offers its own Silk browser, an e-mail client, calendar and contacts apps, and an available Skype app, as well as the Kindle e-reader (see Figure 1-2). In addition, the OfficeSuite productivity apps are built in and include word processor, spreadsheet, and presentation programs.

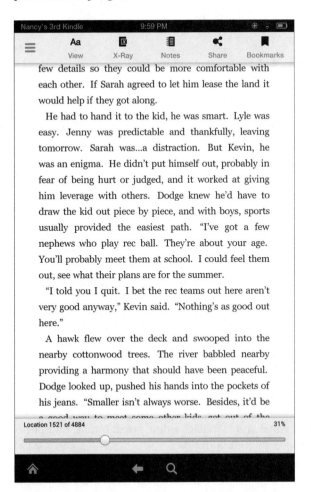

Figure 1-2: Where it all started, with Kindle e-reader functionality.

Just because a particular type of app doesn't come pre-installed on Kindle Fire HDX doesn't mean you can't get one @@you can, and often for free. At this point, the selection of apps available for Android devices isn't nearly as robust as those available for Apple devices, but that will change over time. See Chapter 11 for a list of ten apps that can flesh out your Kindle Fire HDX with popular features such as a budget tracker, weather reporter, and drawing app, and check out Chapter 12 for ten or so great game apps.

Pre-installed functionality

Here's a rundown of the functionality you get out of the box from pre-installed apps:

- E-reader to read both books and periodicals
- Music player
- Video player
- Audiobook player
- Contacts app
- Calendar app
- Docs document reader for Word, PDF, RTF, and HTML format files
- Silk web browser
- Camera and Photos (see Figure 1-3) in which you can view and make edits to photos (such as rotate, change brightness and adjust for red-eye, and crop)
- E-mail client (use this to set up Kindle Fire HDX to access your existing e-mail accounts)
- Integration for Facebook and Twitter
- OfficeSuite for simple word processing and spreadsheet functionality

Check out the apps stored in the Cloud (meaning that these apps are stored at Amazon, rather than pre-installed on your device) by tapping Apps on the Home screen and then tapping the Cloud tab. Here, you may find a number of free apps, such as a Wi-Fi analyzer (to check your Wi-Fi connection), free games, and more.

Here are some of the things you can use your Kindle Fire HDX for:

- Shopping at Amazon for music, video, apps, books, and periodicals, and viewing or playing that content.
- Storing Amazon-purchased content in the Amazon Cloud Drive and playing music and video selections from the Cloud instead of downloading them to your device. Amazon content doesn't count toward your Amazon Cloud Drive storage limit (20GB), but other content backed up there does. Note that you can go to `www.amazon.com/clouddrive`

and purchase anywhere from 20GB for $10 a year up to 1,000GB of storage for $500.

✔ Sending documents to yourself at a Kindle e-mail address that's assigned when you register your device (see Chapter 2 for more about setting up your Kindle Fire HDX, and Chapter 10 for more about using your Kindle Fire e-mail address to send documents to your Kindle Fire HDX).

✔ *Sideloading* (transferring) content from your computer to your Kindle Fire HDX by using a micro USB cable that comes with the tablet. Using this cable (see Figure 1-4), you can copy photos, music, videos, and documents (Word or PDF) from any computer onto your Kindle Fire HDX.

✔ Making video calls using the free Skype for Kindle Fire HDX app.

✔ "Flinging" movies from your device to your large-screen TV using the Second Screen feature.

Figure 1-3: Use the Photos app to view photos and edit them.

Figure 1-4: The Kindle Fire HDX's micro USB cable and a power adapter.

The magic of Whispersync

If you've ever owned a Kindle e-reader, you know that downloading Amazon content to it has always been seamless. All you need for this process is access to a Wi-Fi or 4G network. Then you simply order a book, music, or a video, and within moments, it appears on your Kindle device.

Kindle Fire HDX enjoys the same kind of easy download capability via Amazon's Whispersync technology for books, audiobooks, music, video, and periodicals.

Whispersync also helps sync items such as bookmarks you've placed in e-books or the last place you watched in a video across various devices. For example, say you have the Kindle e-reader app on your Kindle Fire HDX, PC, and smartphone. Wherever you left off reading, whatever notes you entered, and whatever pages you've bookmarked will be synced among all the devices without your having to lift a finger. (See Chapter 6 for details on notes, book-marking, and more features of the e-reader.)

Immersion Reading is a feature that uses Whispersync to allow you to play an audiobook and have the current word that's being spoken highlighted in the text. This feature supposedly aids in reader retention, so it might be a nice match for those late-night study sessions with textbooks.

You want content — Amazon's got it

As I've stated before, Kindle Fire HDX is meant to be a device you use to consume media, meaning that you can use it to play/read all kinds of music, movies, TV shows, podcasts, e-books, audiobooks, magazines, and newspapers. Amazon has built up a huge amount of content, from print (see Figure 1-5) to audio books via its subsidiary Audible (more than 22 million) to movies, TV shows, songs, books, magazines, audiobooks, apps, and games.

Figure 1-5: The Kindle Store offers more than 1 million books for the Kindle e-reader app.

Count on these numbers to have risen by the time you read this: Amazon continues to rack up deals with media groups such as Fox Broadcasting and PBS to make even more content available on a regular basis.

Tap a library — such as Books, Music, or Videos — on the Kindle Fire HDX Home screen, and you can find various kinds of content in the Amazon store by tapping the Store button. Tap Newsstand to shop for periodicals (see Figure 1-6) and Music to shop for songs and albums; tap Video and you go directly to the Amazon Video store. Tap Apps to shop the Amazon Appstore. All the content you purchase is backed up on the Amazon Cloud Drive.

Another form of content that you get for free is the information contained in the IMDb, a database owned by Amazon. This information is used by the X-Ray feature to show you information about actors and characters in videos, song lyrics in music, and characters in books.

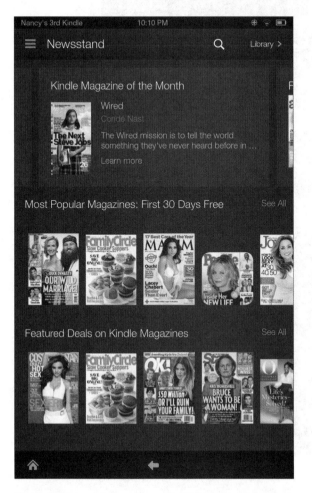

Figure 1-6: Amazon's magazine selection is constantly growing.

When you own a Kindle you can take advantage of the Kindle Owner's Lending Library, where you can choose from more than 200,000 books to borrow at no charge for as long as you like. If you have an Amazon Prime membership, you can also get one free book a month for your permanent library.

If you're concerned about kids who access content over your Kindle Fire HDX, check out the limitations you can place using the FreeTime parental controls (see Chapter 3).

See Chapter 4 for more about buying content and apps for your Kindle Fire HDX.

Browsing with Amazon Silk

Silk is Kindle Fire HDX's browser (see Figure 1-7). Silk is simple to use, but the real benefits of Amazon Silk are all about browsing performance.

Amazon Silk is touted as a "Cloud-accelerated split browser." In plain English, this means that the browser can use the power of Amazon's servers to load the pages of a website quickly. Because parts of the process of loading web pages are handled not on your Kindle Fire HDX but on servers in the Cloud, your pages should display faster.

In addition, you get what's called a *persistent connection,* which means that your tablet is always connected to the Amazon Internet backbone (the routes that data travels to move among networks online) whenever it has access to a Wi-Fi connection.

New with Kindle Fire HDX comes Reading View in the Silk browser, which removes from your browser view all but the written content. In addition, you get easier-to-use navigation tools and content pages that let you view web content by categories, such as Most Visited and Bookmarks. See Chapter 5 for more about using the Silk browser and Reading View.

The Kindle Fire HDX 7-inch and 8.9-inch Wi-Fi models can connect only via Wi-Fi; the 7 inch and 8.9-inch Kindle Fire HDX 4G LTE Wireless models have both Wi-Fi access and 4G LTE access, so they can connect to a cellular network just as your mobile phone does.

Another touted capability of Silk is the way it filters content to deliver it faster. Say you open a news site, such as MSN or CNN. Obviously, millions of others are accessing these pages on the same day. If most of those folks choose to open the Entertainment page after reading the home page of the site, Silk essentially predicts what page you might open next and preloads it. If you choose to go to that page, too, it appears instantly.

Figure 1-7: Amazon Silk offers simple-to-use browsing tools.

But is it private?

There were some early misgivings about privacy and the Silk browser when the original Kindle Fire was released in 2011. Folks were concerned about the fact that Amazon collects information about browsing habits in order to predict what page most folks were likely to browse to next.

These fears were allayed when Amazon assured the press and others that they don't collect personally identifiable information (meaning they note that a user clicked a particular link but don't keep a record of which user did so), nor do they use this information for anything other than to produce a better browsing experience.

A world of color on the display

The display on Kindle Fire HDX offers a high-resolution screen that makes for very crisp colors when you're watching that hit movie or reading a colorful magazine (see Figure 1-8). *In-plane switching* is a technology that gives you a wide viewing angle on the Kindle Fire HDX screen. The result is that if you want to share your movie with a friend sitting next to you on the couch, she'll have no problem seeing what's on the screen from that side angle.

Figure 1-8: The bright display on Kindle Fire HDX makes media shine.

In addition, the screen is coated with layers of gorilla glass that make it extra strong, so it should withstand most of the bumps and scratches you throw at it.

Of course, you should avoid dropping your Kindle Fire HDX, exposing it to extreme temperatures, or spilling liquids on it. The User Guide also advises that if you do spill liquids, you shouldn't heat the device in your microwave to dry it off. (Perhaps a case of tablet maintenance advice for real dummies?)

Understanding the value of Amazon Prime

Kindle Fire HDX comes with one free month of Amazon Prime. I've been an Amazon Prime member for years, so I can tell you firsthand that this service is one of the best deals out there. During your free month, Prime will allow you to get a lot of perks, such as free two-day shipping on thousands of items sold through Amazon, a free e-book, and free instant videos.

If you decide to pick up the service after your free month, it will cost you $79 a year. So, what do you get for your money?

Prime includes free two-day shipping on millions of items and overnight shipping for only a few dollars more. Not every item offered on Amazon is eligible for Prime, but enough are that it's a wonderful savings in time and money over the course of a year. You can probably pay for the membership with the free shipping on the first two or three orders you place. And getting your Prime stuff in only two days every time is sweet.

Figure 1-9: The Prime Instant Videos service adds new videos all the time; check it out!

In addition, Prime membership gives you access to Prime Instant Videos (see Figure 1-9), which includes thousands of movies and TV shows that can be streamed to your Kindle Fire HDX absolutely free. We're not talking obscure 1970s sleepers here: Recent additions to Prime Instant Videos include TV shows such as *Downton Abbey* and *Parks and Recreation,* and award-winning movies such as *Rango* and *True Grit.*

If you have already paid for a yearly subscription to Amazon Prime, you don't get an extra month for free, sad to say. And if you don't have a Prime account, your 30 days of a free account starts from the time you activate your Kindle Fire HDX, not the first time you make a Prime purchase or stream a Prime Instant Video. So, my suggestion is to start using it right away to take full advantage and decide whether the paid membership is for you.

2

Kindle Fire HDX Quickstart

In This Chapter

▶ Setting up your Kindle Fire HDX

▶ Playing with libraries, the Carousel, and Favorites

▶ Transferring data from your PC or Mac

▶ Getting help with Amazon Assist

*T*he basics of using Kindle Fire HDX are. . . well, pretty basic. You start by turning it on and following a set of extremely short and simple instructions to set it up and register it, and then you can begin to get acquainted with its features.

In this chapter, I help you to get familiar with what comes in the box, explore the interface (what you see on the screen), and start to use your fingers to interact with the touchscreen. To round out your introduction to Kindle Fire HDX basics, you begin to get a sense of how things are organized on Kindle Fire HDX's Home screen and learn how to use the new Amazon Assist help feature.

Get Going with Kindle Fire HDX

There's always a logical place to start building a fire. In this case, forget the logs and matches, and get started by examining what comes in the Kindle Fire HDX box and learn how to turn your new tablet on and off. The first time you turn on Kindle Fire HDX, you register it and link it to your Amazon account so you can shop till you drop.

Also, although your device probably comes with a decent battery charge, at some point, you'll inevitably have to charge the battery, so I cover that in the section "Charging the battery," later in this chapter.

Opening the box

When your Kindle Fire HDX arrives, it will come in a dark gray box in a sleeve that sports the image of the Kindle Home screen (see Figure 2-1). The Kindle Fire HDX rests on top of a piece of orange cardboard, with a black card that contains some Kindle Fire HDX basics printed on both sides. Finally, above the Kindle Fire HDX is a black box containing a micro USB cable that you use to connect the device to a computer and charge the Kindle Fire. That's it.

Remove the protective plastic from the device, and you're ready to get going.

Turning your Kindle Fire HDX on and off

After you get the tablet out of its packaging, it's time to turn it on. The Kindle Fire HDX sports a Power button on the back near the top when you hold it in portrait orientation (see Figure 2-2). On the back near the bottom is the volume rocker, as well as a headphone jack. On the top edge of the device is a micro USB port, where you can insert the micro USB cable to connect the Kindle Fire HDX to your computer or an outlet to charge it.

Figure 2-1: The Kindle Fire HDX packaging.

Micro USB port   Power button

Headphone jack   Volume rocker

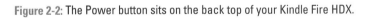

Figure 2-2: The Power button sits on the back top of your Kindle Fire HDX.

To turn the device on, press the Power button on the back. If you're starting up for the first time, you're taken through a series of setup screens (see "Setting Up Your Kindle Fire HDX," later in this chapter, for more about this). After you go through the setup process and register your Kindle Fire HDX, you'll see the Home screen shown in Figure 2-3 on startup.

The Status bar gives you information about items such as your device's battery charge, as well as access to a Quick Settings menu for universal Kindle Fire HDX settings; the list of Libraries (Games, Apps, and so on) provides access to libraries of content and related Amazon stores. In the middle of the screen is a carousel of your most recently used content and apps, and along the bottom is a grid of Favorite apps (the Silk browser, Mail, Help, and so on). You can find more about the elements on the Home screen in the section "Getting to Know the Interface," later in this chapter.

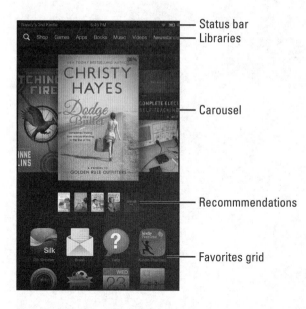

— Status bar
— Libraries

— Carousel

— Recommmendations

— Favorites grid

Figure 2-3: The Kindle Fire HDX Home screen.

If you want to lock your Kindle Fire HDX, which is akin to putting a laptop computer to sleep, press the Power button. To shut down your Kindle, from any screen (except the Lock screen) press and hold the Power button until a message appears offering you the options to Power Off or Cancel, as shown in Figure 2-4.

If your Kindle Fire HDX becomes nonresponsive, you can press and hold the Power button for 20 seconds, and it should come to life again.

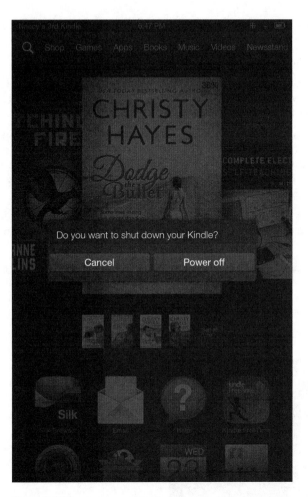

Figure 2-4: You can proceed to shut down your device,
or cancel and return to the Home screen.

If you own an original Kindle Fire or Kindle Fire HD, you'll find the Power
button, micro USB port, and headset jack ports in different locations than on
the HDX.

Getting to know the touchscreen

Before you work through the setup screens for your Kindle Fire HDX, it
will help if you to get to know the basics of navigating the touchscreen —
especially if you've never used a touchscreen before:

- Swipe down from the Status bar at the top of the Home screen to display Quick Settings and Notifications (such as download status and
e-mail messages in your Inbox); swipe up to hide the Quick Settings and
Notifications.

✓ Tap the Home button (shaped like a little house) at any time to return to the Home screen.

✓ Tap an item to select it or open it.

✓ If your Kindle Fire HDX goes to a lock screen after a period of inactivity, tap the Power button and then swipe the Unlock button (see Figure 2-5) from right to left to go to the Home screen.

✓ Double-tap the screen to enlarge text, and double-tap again to return the text to its original size. *Note:* This works only in certain locations, such as when displaying a web page in the Silk browser. Double-tapping in some other locations, such as when reading a book or viewing a video, will display tools.

✓ Place your fingers apart on a screen and pinch them together to zoom out on the current view; place your fingers together on the screen and then move them apart (unpinch) to enlarge the view.

✓ Swipe left to move to the next page in the e-reader. Swipe to the right to move to the previous page in a book. In many other apps, swiping to the right will display the Navigation panel, offering options for moving around the app's screens.

✓ Swipe up and down to scroll up and down a web page.

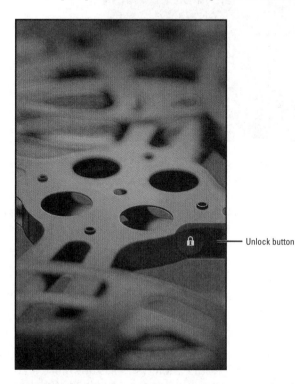

Unlock button

Figure 2-5: Swipe the Unlock button to go to the Home screen.

These touchscreen gestures will help you get around most of the content and setup screens you encounter in Kindle Fire HDX.

If you prefer to use your Kindle Fire HDX and its touchscreen without holding the device in your hands, consider getting the new Oragami cover, which you can use as a stand for your Kindle Fire. Ranging from $50 to $65, depending on whether you opt for leather or a less expensive option, this clever cover not only protects your Kindle Fire but also acts as a useful stand to hold it upright while you work with it.

Setting up your Kindle Fire HDX

When you turn Kindle Fire HDX on for the first time, you see a series of screens that help you set up and register the device. Don't worry: There aren't many questions, and you know all the answers.

At some point during this setup procedure, you may be prompted to plug your adapter in if your battery charge is low. You may also be notified that the latest Kindle software is downloading and have to wait for that process to complete before you can move forward.

The first choice you have is which language your Kindle Fire HDX should use. Tap the language to use from the provided list and then tap the Continue button.

This is the point in the setup process at which you connect to a Wi-Fi network. You need this connection to register your device (if Amazon hasn't already preregistered your device to your account). Follow these steps to register and set up your Kindle Fire HDX:

1. **In the Connect to Wi-Fi list (shown on the screen in Figure 2-6), tap an available network.**

   Kindle Fire HDX connects to the network (you may need to enter a password and then tap Connect to access an available network).

2. **On the Register Your Kindle screen that appears, enter your Amazon account information, e-mail address, and a password in the appropriate fields, and then skip to Step 5; if you don't have an Amazon account, see Step 3.**

   If Amazon has preregistered your account to the device, at this point you can deregister it and register to a different account (see Figure 2-7), or tap Continue and move to Step 4.

3. **If you don't have an Amazon account, click the New to Amazon? Create Account link.**

   This link takes you to the Create an Amazon Account screen (see Figure 2-8, with fields for entering your name, e-mail address, and password (which you have to retype to confirm).

4. **Enter this information and then tap Continue, accepting any terms or conditions when they appear.**

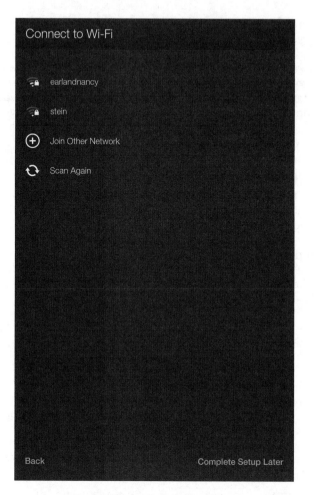

Figure 2-6: Start by connecting to a Wi-Fi network.

5. **On the next screen, shown in Figure 2-9, you can tap the social networking services Facebook and Twitter and enter your account information for each service (one at a time).**

   You can also set up these accounts later by swiping down to display Quick Settings and then tapping Settings — My Account — Social Network Account.

6. **In the Welcome to Kindle Fire screen that appears (see Figure 2-10), tap Get Started.**

At this point you see the first of several screens that help you learn to navigate Kindle Fire HDX by swiping left, up, and down on its screen (see Figure 2-11). At the end of the series, on the screen titled Congratulations, tap Finish to go to the Kindle Fire Home screen.

Figure 2-7: You have to register your Kindle Fire HDX to use it.

When you register your Kindle Fire HDX to your Amazon account, a Kindle Fire e-mail address is created. You can use this e-mail address to send or have other people send documents to you, which then appear in your Docs library on your Kindle Fire HDX, or photos, which appear in your Photos app. See Chapter 10 for more about working with Docs.

Charging the battery

According to various media sources that have benchmarked Kindle Fire HDX's performance, it has a battery life of about 11 hours for Wi-Fi–connected activities, such as web browsing, streaming movies, and listening to music from the Cloud. If you're a bookworm who's more into the printed word than media, you'll be happy to hear that Amazon claims you get about 17 hours of reading downloaded books with Wi-Fi turned off.

amazon   Your Account | Help

Registration
New to Amazon.com? Register Below.

My name is: [   ]

My e-mail address is: [   ]

Type it again: [   ]

My mobile phone number is: [   ] (Optional)
Learn more

Protect your information with a password
This will be your only Amazon.com password.

Enter a new password: [   ]

Type it again: [   ]

[Create account]

By creating an account, you agree to Amazon.com's Conditions of Use and Privacy Notice.

Conditions of Use Privacy Notice © 1996-2013, Amazon.com, Inc. or its affiliates

Figure 2-8: Create a new account by entering a few details.

You charge the battery by using the provided micro USB cable and power adapter. Attach the smaller end of the micro USB cable to your Kindle Fire HDX's micro USB port, located along the top of the device when held in portrait orientation (refer to Figure 2-2), and the other end of the micro USB cable into the power adapter, which you then plug into a wall outlet. If Kindle Fire HDX is completely out of juice, it will take about four to six hours to charge it.

A battery indicator on the Status bar runs across the top of the Kindle Fire HDX screen; you can check this to see if your battery is running low. The more white there is in the little battery icon, the more battery time you have left. The left side of the icon turns red when the battery is very low.

Getting to Know the Interface

The interface you see on the Kindle Home screen (see Figure 2-12) is made up of four items. At the top is the Status bar, which includes indicators that tell you:

- The name of your Kindle Fire
- The time
- Whether you're in Airplane mode or connected to a network
- Remaining battery life

Figure 2-9: Choose the social networking accounts you want
to use.

Next, you see a set of buttons that take you to the Kindle Fire HDX libraries
that contain various types of content such as Books, Videos, Games, Apps,
and Audiobooks. This row also contains a button to shop at the Amazon
Store, open the Silk browser by tapping Web, view Photos or Docs, and look
at special offers.

In the middle of the screen is the Carousel. The Carousel contains images of
items you recently used that you can flick with your finger to scroll through
and tap any item to open it. The item on top is the most recently viewed item,
and others are shown in the chronological order in which you last used them.
When you scroll and display an item, Amazon's recommendations for similar
content are displayed in thumbnails underneath (except for Docs).

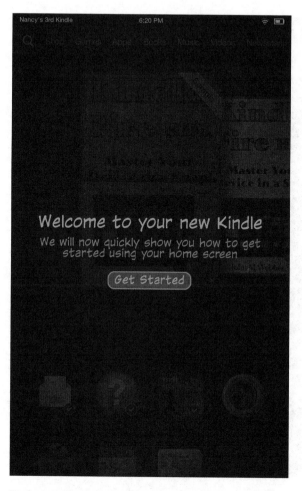

Figure 2-10: You're ready to get going with Kindle Fire HDX.

Finally, underneath the item on the Carousel that is front and center is a listing of recommendations for similar items based on your buying habits.

Accessing Kindle Fire HDX libraries

Kindle Fire HDX libraries are where you access downloaded content, as well as content stored by Amazon in the Cloud. Libraries (with the exception of the Docs and Photos libraries) also offer a Store button that you can tap to go online to browse and buy more content.

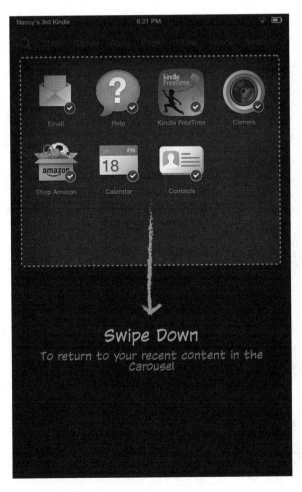

Figure 2-11: This very quick tutorial covers the basics of using Kindle Fire HDX.

Tap any library button to open a library of downloaded and archived content: Games, Apps, Books, Music, Videos, Newsstand, or Audiobooks. Tap one of these and you'll see a Store button to take you to the associated Amazon store. The Videos button works a bit differently in that it opens to the Amazon Store rather than a library, and you can tap the Library button to go to your library. This difference is due to the fact that, in most cases, it's not very prudent to download a lot of video content to your Kindle Fire HDX because this type of content takes up so much of your device's memory. It's preferable to play video from Amazon's Cloud (which is called *streaming*).

There's also a Web button in among the list of libraries that you can tap to open the Silk web browser. Find out more about going online and using the browser in Chapter 5.

Figure 2-12: This graphical interface is fun to move around with the flick of a finger.

Understanding the Cloud and Kindle Fire HDX

Everything you buy using Kindle Fire HDX's features is purchased through Amazon or its affiliates on the Amazon site. That content is downloaded to your device through a technology called Whispersync, which requires a Wi-Fi connection unless you have the Kindle Fire HD or HDX 4G LTE Wireless model.

When you purchase content, you can choose whether to keep it in the Amazon Cloud or download it to your Kindle Fire HDX. If you download it, you can access it whether or not you're in range of a Wi-Fi network. At any time, you can remove content from the device, and it will be archived in the Cloud for you to stream to your device (music or video) or redownload (music, video, books, and magazines) anytime you like. Keeping content you're not currently using in the Amazon Cloud can save space on your device.

Figure 2-13: Your Music library provides access to all your musical content.

In a library, such as the Music library shown in Figure 2-13, you can tap the On Device or Cloud tab located in the top of the screen. The On Device tab shows you only content you have downloaded; the Cloud tab displays all your purchases or free content stored in Amazon's Cloud library, including content you've downloaded to the Kindle Fire HDX.

You can download archived content to your device at any time or remove downloaded content to the Cloud. You can also view the contents of libraries in different ways, depending on which library you're in. For example, you can view Music library contents by categories such as Songs, Artists, and Albums.

See Chapter 4 for more about buying content, Chapter 6 for information about reading books and magazines, and Chapters 7 and 8, respectively, for more about playing music and video.

It's possible to download video, which is useful if you'll be out of range of a Wi-Fi connection, but I recommend that you remove the content from your device when you're done watching and back in Wi-Fi range. Removing content from Kindle Fire HDX involves finding it in a library, pressing it with your finger, and choosing Remove from Device from the menu that appears.

As mentioned before, you can also sideload content you've obtained from other sources, such as iTunes, to your Kindle Fire HD libraries. *Sideloading* involves connecting the micro USB cable that came with your Kindle Fire HDX to your computer (with the power adapter removed) and then copying content to Kindle Fire HDX. See the section "Using a Micro USB Cable to Transfer Data," later in this chapter, for more about this process.

Playing with the Carousel

Many of us have fond memories of riding a carousel at the fair as kids. The Kindle Fire HDX Carousel may not bring the same thrill, but it does have its charms as you swipe through it to see a revolving display of recently used books, audiobooks, music, videos, websites, docs, and apps (see Figure 2-14).

If you've used an Android smartphone, you may have encountered the Carousel concept. On Kindle Fire HDX, items you've used recently are displayed here chronologically, with the item you used most recently on top. You can swipe your finger to the right or left to flick through the Carousel contents. When you find an item you want to view or play, tap it to open it.

Whatever you tap opens in the associated player or reader. Music will open in the Amazon MP3 music player; video in the Amazon Video player; and docs, books, and magazines in the Kindle e-reader.

In addition to using the Carousel to view content and apps, you can use Quickswitch, a new feature that allows you to swipe up from the bottom of any screen other than the Home screen to see a scrollable list of content and apps, kind of like a visual table of contents for your Kindle Fire. Scroll to the right or left to find an item and tap it to open it.

Getting on the grid

When you're on a roll using Kindle Fire HDX for accessing all kinds of content, the Carousel, which contains recently viewed content or apps, can get a bit crowded. You may have to swipe five or six times to find what you need. That's where Favorites comes in.

The concept of Favorites is probably familiar to you from working with web browsers, in which Favorites is a feature that allows you to put websites you visit frequently in a Favorites folder. On the Kindle Fire HDX, Favorites is also a place for saving frequently used content and apps that takes the form of a grid of thumbnails at the bottom of the Home screen.

Figure 2-14: Kindle Fire HDX's Carousel makes recently used content available.

If, for example, you're reading a book you open often or you play a certain piece of music frequently, place it in the Favorites area of the Kindle Fire HDX, and you can find it more quickly.

By default, Favorites includes commonly used apps in its top two rows, including:

- ✔ The Silk browser
- ✔ The E-mail app
- ✔ Help & Support
- ✔ Kindle FreeTime
- ✔ The Camera

- ✔ Shop Amazon
- ✔ Calendar
- ✔ Contacts

To pin an item to Favorites, press and hold it in the Carousel or a library, and then tap Add to Home from the menu that appears (see Figure 2-15).

To remove content from Favorites, press and hold an item in the grid. The Remove button appears. You can tap additional items if you like and then tap Remove (see Figure 2-16). Though deleted from the Favorites grid, items are still available to you on the Carousel and in the related library.

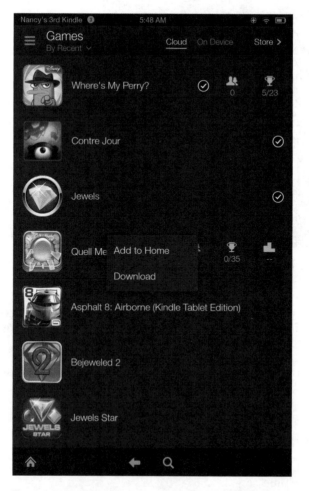

Figure 2-15: Pin items to your Home screen by using this menu.

Figure 2-16: Tap Remove to get rid of selected Favorites.

Getting clues from the Status bar

The Status bar runs across the top of every Kindle Fire HDX screen, just like the Status bar on your mobile phone. This bar, shown in Figure 2-17, provides information about your device name, the time, your network connection, and your battery charge.

Here's a rundown of what you'll find on the Status bar:

✔ **Device name:** First is the name of your Kindle Fire, such as Nancy's Kindle or Nancy's 2nd Kindle.

✔ **Notifications:** A number sometimes appears just to the right of the device name to indicate that you have that many Notifications.

Notifications can come from the Kindle Fire HDX system announcing a completed download, or the e-mail client announcing that a new e-mail has arrived, for example. To view all your notifications, swipe down from the Status bar, and a list appears (see Figure 2-18).

✔ **Current time:** The item in the middle of the Status bar is the current time, based on the time zone you specified when setting up the Kindle Fire HDX.

✔ **Wireless:** The item on the Status bar to the right of the time is an icon showing you the Wi-Fi connection status. If this is lit up, you're connected. The more bars in the symbol that are bright white, the stronger the connection.

✔ **Airplane Mode/Bluetooth:** This icon appears when either Airplane Mode or Bluetooth is turned on and displays in a blue color when another Bluetooth device is connected.

Figure 2-17: The various tools and settings available on the Status bar.

✔ **Battery charge:** Finally, the battery icon on the far-right side of the Status bar indicates the percentage of charge remaining on your battery.

You can swipe down from the top of the screen to access Quick Settings. Quick Settings (see Figure 2-19) offer the most commonly used settings. Use these items to turn the Auto-Rotate feature on or off (if it's on, when you turn your Kindle Fire the screen moves around with its orientation), adjust screen brightness, set up your Wi-Fi connection, and turn Quiet Time on or off. Tap the Mayday button to contact an Amazon tech advisor. To access the full Kindle Fire HDX Settings menu, tap Settings on the right of the Quick Settings bar. See Chapter 3 for a detailed breakdown of all Kindle Fire HDX settings.

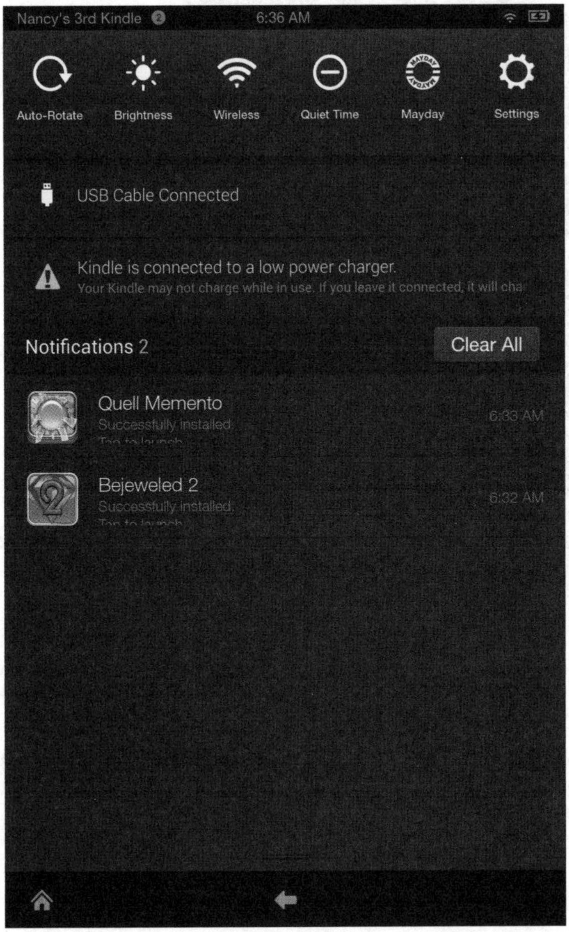

Figure 2-18: The list of current notifications that you can display from any screen.

Figure 2-19: Use the items on the Quick Settings menu or tap Settings to access the full complement of settings for Kindle Fire HDX.

To use Mayday, tap the button on Quick Settings, and on the following screen, tap Connect. In a few seconds (about 15 or so, depending on how busy the folks are) a small window appears in the bottom-right corner with the image of your tech advisor in it. Start asking questions and let the advisor explain, circle items on your screen, or even take over your device and perform procedures for you.

The often-present, ever-changing Options bar

The Options bar runs along the bottom or right side of your Kindle Fire HDX screen, depending on which app or library you open. In some apps, the Options bar is always visible; if the Options bar is hidden, you will typically see a small black tab with lines on it, either on the right side or at the bottom of the screen, which you can swipe to display the Options bar. In other cases (as in the e-reader app), just tap the screen and the Options bar appears.

The items offered on the Options bar change, depending on what library or app you're using, but they always include a Home button. Also, there are often buttons such as Search to run a search in areas such as a content library, and a back arrow to move back one screen. In addition, you'll often see a Menu button when you tap the Options bar. This icon, which looks like a little box with three lines in it, makes available commonly used settings for the currently displayed feature, such as a button to switch to list view rather than thumbnails. Figure 2-20 shows you the options available on the Newsstand library screen. From left to right in the figure, these buttons are Home, back arrow, Menu, and Search.

Figure 2-20: The Options bar offers contextually relevant options, depending on which app is displayed.

Use the Home button to jump back to the Kindle Fire HDX Home screen from anywhere. On some screens where it would be annoying to be distracted by the Options bar, such as the e-reader, you may have to tap the screen to make the Options bar appear.

The Navigation panel

New with Fire OS 3.0 is a Navigation panel that appears in some apps. You access this panel by swiping to the right from the edge of the screen, or you can tap the Left Nav button instead. The Left Nav button is the one containing three lines stacked on top of each other; you'll find it in the top-left corner of the screen.

The Navigation panel, shown in Figure 2-21, contains different options based on what app or content you're working with. For example, in a book, the Navigation panel displays a list of articles; in the Silk browser, it provides shortcuts labeled Bookmarks, Most Visited Sites, Downloads, and more.

Using a Micro USB Cable to Transfer Data

It's easy to purchase or rent content from Amazon, which you can choose to download directly to your Kindle Fire HDX or stream from the Amazon Cloud. However, you may want to get content from other places, such as iTunes or your Pictures folder on your computer, and play or view it on your Kindle Fire HDX.

To transfer content to Kindle Fire HDX, you use the micro USB cable that came with your tablet. This cable has a USB connector on one end that you can plug into your PC or Mac, and a micro USB connector on the other that fits into the micro USB port on your Kindle Fire HDX (which is located on the top near the Power button when holding Kindle Fire HDX in portrait orientation; refer to Figure 2-2).

Attach the micro USB end to your Kindle Fire HDX (see Figure 2-22) and the USB end to your computer. Your Kindle Fire HDX should then appear as a drive in File Explorer in Windows 8 or later (see Figure 2-23) or the Mac Finder. You can now click and drag files from your hard drive to the Kindle Fire HDX or use the copy and paste functions to accomplish the same thing.

Using this process, you can transfer apps, photos, docs, music, e-books, audiobooks, and videos from your computer to your Kindle Fire HDX. Then, just tap the relevant library (such as Books for e-books and Music for songs) to read or play the content on your Kindle Fire HDX.

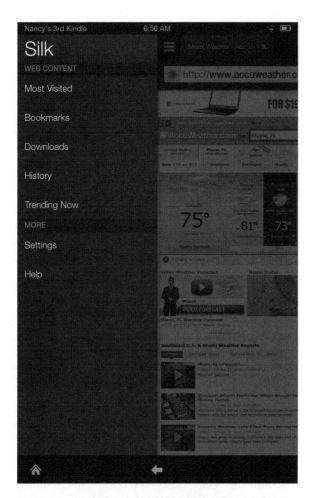

Figure 2-21: Choices here change based on what app or content you're viewing.

Figure 2-22: Connecting the micro USB cable to Kindle Fire HDX.

Figure 2-23: Kindle Fire HDX contents shown as a drive in File Explorer.

You can also upload content to your Amazon Cloud Drive on your computer, and that content will then be available on your Kindle Fire HDX. Go to Amazon.com, search for Cloud Drive Installer, download the app, and then use the app to access your Cloud Drive on your computer and manage the drive's contents.

You can share photos via e-mail, Facebook, or Twitter. Tap Photos on the Home screen, locate a photo, and press and hold it. On the menu that appears, tap Share and then choose the method of sharing. Fill out the e-mail, Facebook, or Twitter form that appears and tap Send or Post. Using this method, you can share with yourself or others. You will find Share features in several apps; for example, in the Silk browser, tap the menu on the Options bar and tap Share Page to share the current page's URL.

3

Kindle Fire HDX Settings

In This Chapter

▶ Opening your Kindle Fire HDX's settings

▶ Working with Quick Settings

▶ Delving into all the settings Kindle Fire HDX offers

*W*hen you first take your Kindle Fire HDX out of the box, Amazon has provided you with default settings that will work for most people most of the time. However, we've all gotten used to being able to personalize our experience with phone and computer devices, so you may be curious about the various ways in which you can make Kindle Fire HDX work uniquely for you.

A tablet device such as Kindle Fire HDX has dozens of settings that help you manage your tablet experience. Some of these settings are discussed in the chapters that cover individual apps, such as the Amazon video player (Chapter 8) and Contacts (Chapter 9). But you may need to review other settings when you start using your Kindle Fire HDX. I cover those more general settings in this chapter.

Opening Quick Settings

In this fast-paced day and age, quick is the name of the game for most of us, so Amazon has provided you with Quick Settings to streamline your settings experience.

You access both a short list of commonly used settings (Quick Settings) and all the more detailed settings for Kindle Fire HDX by swiping downward from the top of the screen.

Figure 3-1 shows the settings that you can control from the Quick Settings menu, each of which is described in the following sections.

Controlling spin with Auto-Rotate

When you turn your Kindle Fire HDX around, the screen automatically rotates from a portrait orientation to a landscape orientation, depending on how you're holding it at the moment. This is great if you decide you want to slip to a different orientation in some apps to see your content more easily. However, if you don't want the orientation to keep flipping whenever you move the device, you can turn off the Auto-Rotate feature. This is handy, for example, when you're lying on the beach reading a book and don't want it to flip to another orientation every time you turn to even out your suntan.

Figure 3-1: Quick Settings control the settings that you access most often.

To toggle this feature on or off, tap this setting in Quick Settings to toggle between Auto-Rotate, which lets you freely rotate as you move it into different orientations, and Locked, which locks the screen in its current orientation.

Turning up the Brightness

By turning up the screen brightness on your Kindle Fire, you may be able to see items more clearly. However, you should be aware that a higher brightness setting can eat up your battery power more quickly.

You can tap the Brightness setting in Quick Settings to display the Auto-Brightness On/Off button to turn on or off a feature that controls the brightness of the screen based on ambient light. You can also use the slider above this setting (see Figure 3-2) to adjust the brightness manually.

Figure 3-2: Adjust brightness manually by using this slider.

Flying high with Airplane Mode

Airplane Mode is a setting you should use if you're flying on a plane. With this off, your device won't search for available networks and could conflict with airplane communications.

To toggle Airplane Mode on and off, in Quick Settings, tap Wireless to display the Airplane Mode On/Off button. With Airplane Mode set to On, no available networks appear. Tap Wi-Fi and tap the On button, and a list of available networks appears (see Figure 3-3). Tap an available network to join it. Note that you may be asked to enter a password to access some networks. For more on Wireless settings, see the section "Setting up Wireless and Networks," later in this chapter.

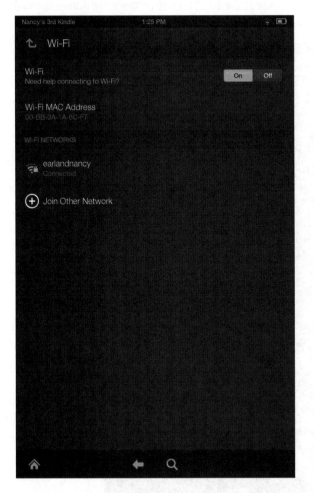

Figure 3-3: Choose from the list of available networks.

Relaxing with Quiet Time

We all have times when we need to concentrate or relax, and at times like these, those little beeps and rings that come with notifications on your Kindle Fire can be, frankly, annoying.

Toggle the Quiet Time setting on and off, depending on whether you want to hear notification sounds and view notification pop-ups. When this setting is off, all those annoying sounds go away.

Sending out a Mayday

The hottest new help feature in HDX is Amazon Assist, which provides a live support person who can walk you through a solution to your problem, take control of your screen and make changes or settings for you, or draw on your screen to show you what to do.

The technical advisor can't see you, though you can see him or her in a small window on your screen (see Figure 3-4). You can pause the Mayday transmission if you need to type in a password so the support person can't see your screen when you do. Both you and the support person have the ability to drag the small window containing his or her image around your screen so that you can see whatever you need to be working with on the screen.

Figure 3-4: Help is a tap away with Mayday.

Mayday is available 7 days a week, 365 days of the year. Tap the Mayday button in Quick Settings (see Figure 3-5) and then tap the Connect button that appears to connect to Amazon Assist. It usually takes about 15 seconds for somebody to appear. If that person can't answer your question, he or she may put you on hold while checking with somebody else for an answer or testing the feature themselves. Currently there is no time limit to how long you can stay on a Mayday call nor how many calls you can make. However, it remains to be seen whether Amazon can keep up with that level of support, and how many people might abuse the system to bend somebody's ear or test Amazon's patience.

Figure 3-5: Tap this button to get help in seconds.

Finding Other Settings

Beyond what I discuss in the preceding section, there's one more item on the Quick Settings menu — Settings. Figure 3-6 shows you the many settings that appear when you tap the Settings button.

These settings include Sync All Content, My Account, Help, Parental Controls, Device, Wireless, Applications, Notifications & Quiet Time, Display & Sounds, Keyboards, Accessibility, Security, Legal & Compliance.

You won't need to change many of these settings very often because the way Kindle Fire HDX works out of the box is usually very intuitive. But if you do find that you want to make an adjustment to settings such as the date and time or parental controls, it's useful to know what's available.

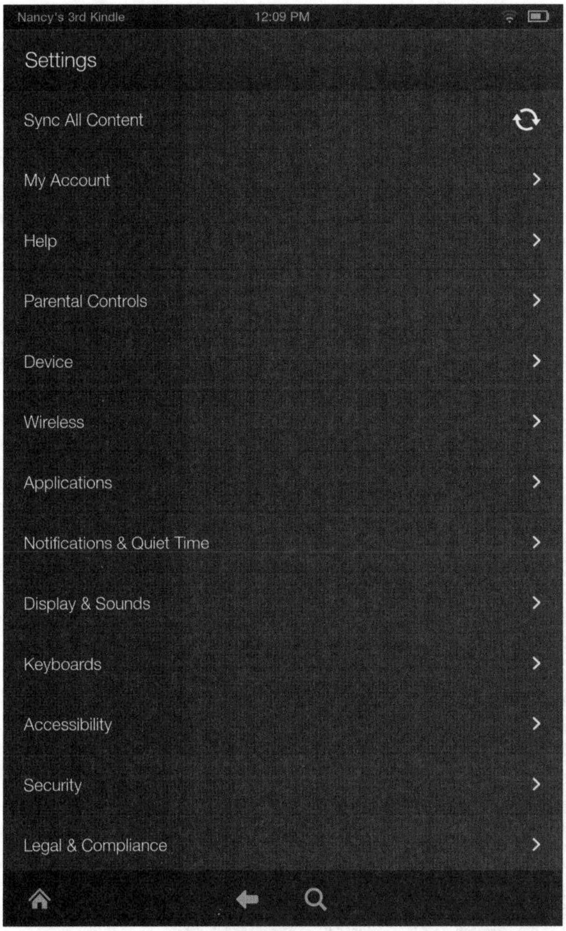

Figure 3-6: Plenty more settings are revealed when you tap Settings.

The following sections give you the skinny on what settings appear when you tap Settings in the Quick Settings menu.

Sync All Content

If you've been away from a network and now have a connection, you can tap the Sync All Content setting to sync any content you might have acquired while offline.

My Account

Kindle Fire HDX does much of what it does by accessing your Amazon account. You need to have an Amazon account to shop, access the Amazon Cloud Drive library online, and register your Kindle Fire HDX, for example.

The My Account option in Settings provides information about the account to which the device is registered (see Figure 3-7). To view your Kindle e-mail address, tap the Learn More About Your Kindle Email Address link. To remove this account from your Kindle Fire HDX, from the My Account screen, tap the Deregister button. Because the obvious thing to do next is to register your Kindle Fire HDX to another account (because so much depends on your having an associated account), you then are presented with a Register button. Tap Register and fill in your Amazon username and password to register the device.

If you deregister your account, don't register your Kindle Fire HDX, and leave this screen, you're placed in the introductory demo that appeared when you first set up your Kindle Fire HDX. When you finish that demo and tap any category, such as Books, you're again prompted to register your device to your Amazon account.

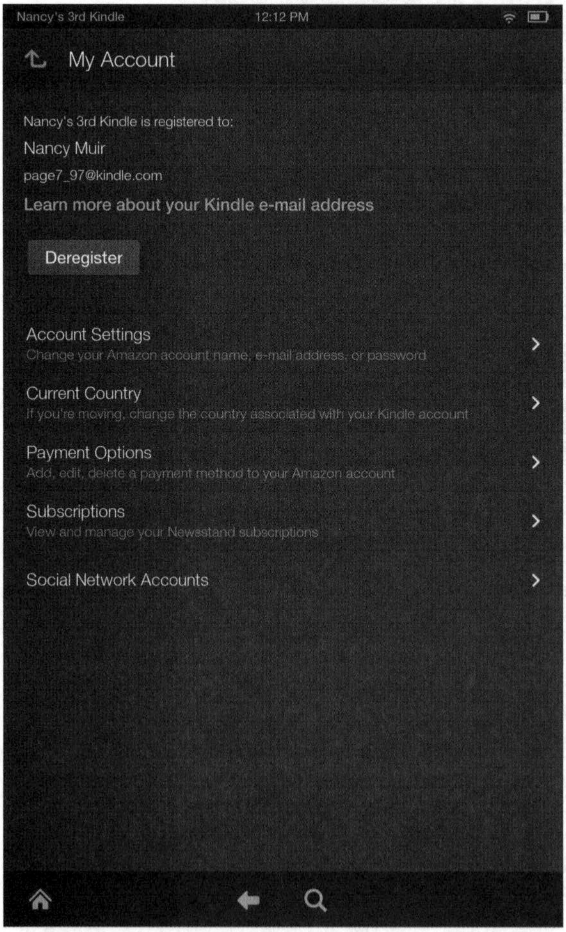

Figure 3-7: Check which Amazon account your device is registered to.

The My Account screen also offers the option of managing social networking accounts and your Amazon account, your current country, subscriptions, and payment options.

Tap the Social Network Accounts link to set up your Twitter and Facebook accounts so that you can take advantage of built-in features for sharing information via either service. Tap the Account Settings link to manage your Amazon account name, e-mail address, and password.

Help

Now and then, we all need a bit of help, and when you're first using a new device such as Kindle Fire HDX, you should know where to find that help (on the off chance that you don't have this book handy).

When you tap Settings from Quick Settings and then tap Help, you see the Help screen (see Figure 3-8), which offers a world of support and allows you to interact with Amazon customer service.

The Help screen includes four options: Amazon Assist Connect button, Wireless help, User Guide, and Contact Us. Here's how all four options work:

- ✔ **Amazon Assist:** Tapping this Connect button is another way to connect to the Amazon Assist feature (the other being the Mayday button in Quick Settings). Once you're connected, an Amazon tech advisor will walk you through any procedure you have questions about.

- ✔ **Wireless:** Use this feature to get help with and troubleshoot your wireless connections, including Wi-Fi and Bluetooth.

- ✔ **User Guide:** The User Guide (see Figure 3-9) offers more comprehensive help on a few dozen topics such as using Kindle FreeTime, watching movies and listening to music, and playing games.

- ✔ **Contact Us:** This selection leads to two topics: Customer Service and Feedback.

  To use Customer Service:

  1. *Tap Customer Service and then tap the Select an Issue field.*

  2. *Choose from the list that appears (containing items such as Newsstand, Books, Docs, and so on).*

  3. *Tap the Select Issue Details field and then tap to select your type of issue from the list that appears.*

  4. *Tap the E-mail or Phone button to view either an email form you can fill out and send or a form where you can enter your phone number and tap a Call Me Now button to receive a phone call.???*

Figure 3-8: Help settings for Kindle Fire HDX.

To use Feedback:

1. *Tap Feedback and select a feature.*

2. *Enter your comment in the Tell Us What You Think about This Feature field (see Figure 3-10).*

   You can also tap one to five stars to rate the feature you're providing feedback on.

3. *Tap the Send Feedback button to submit your thoughts to Amazon.*

Parental Controls

With Fire OS 3.0, the operating system for the Kindle Fire HDX, parental controls include FreeTime. FreeTime allows you to make settings to limit how long kids can read, use apps, or watch video.

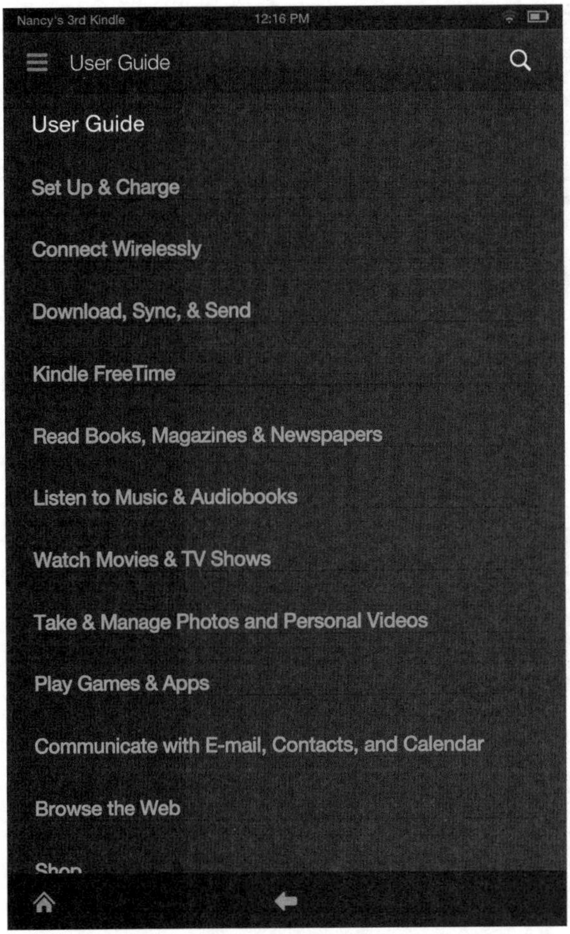

Figure 3-9: The User Guide offers you help on a variety of topics.

When you turn on the Parental Controls setting, you're first presented with the fields for entering and confirming a password. When you've entered your Parental Controls password, tap Finish. Note that once you have created this password, whenever you go into Parental Controls and enter that password you tap Submit to proceed.

In the screen that opens (see Figure 3-11), tap to unblock the Web Browser or E-Mail, Contacts, Social Sharing, and Camera settings. You can also tap to password-protect purchases or video playback. If you want to allow or block certain types of content, scroll down and tap Block and Unblock Content Types; then tap the content you want to block, such as Music, Video, or Apps and Games.

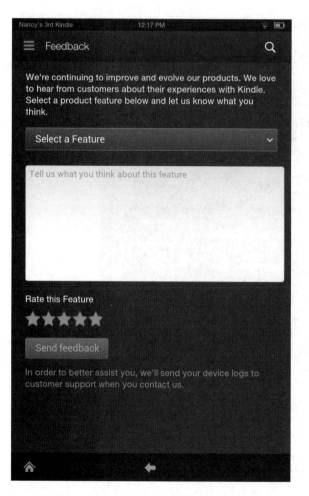

Figure 3-10: The Feedback feature of Help & Feedback gives you the ability to rate features of Kindle Fire HDX and provide comments.

Finally, you can tap to turn on or off the Password Protect Wi-Fi feature. When this feature is on, anybody using your Kindle Fire HDX has to enter a password to make an online connection. You can also tap to turn on or off the Password Protect LBS setting to make it mandatory for somebody to enter a password to turn on Location Based Services.

If you turn on location-based services, you're sharing very private information about your whereabouts. If you're concerned about what apps have access to your location, check out those apps in the Amazon Appstore to see whether the permissions listed on their details page mention use of location information.

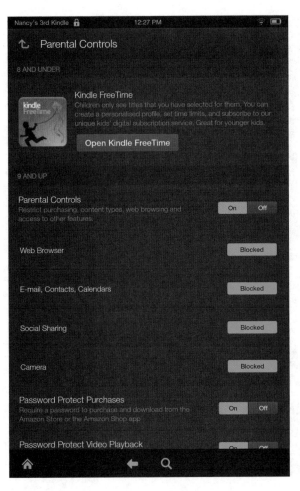

Figure 3-11: Choose what to block or unblock here.

Looking at device settings

You can check your Kindle Fire HDX's Device settings (see Figure 3-12) to find out facts such as the remaining storage space available or your device's serial number. This is also where you can reset your Kindle Fire HDX to the state it was in when it left the factory, if you like a clean slate now and then.

Here are the Device settings available to you:

✔ **Battery:** Indicates the percentage of battery power remaining. Tap the next item down, Show Battery Percentage in Status Bar, if you want to see the numerical percentage next to the battery icon that always appears at the top-right corner of the screen.

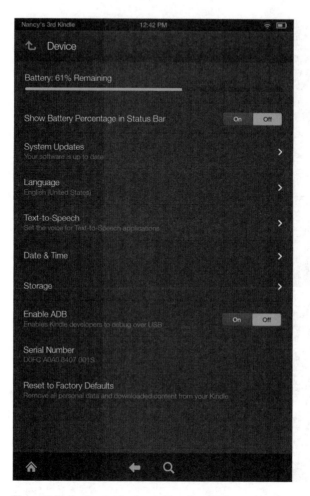

Figure 3-12: Device settings provide a lot of information about the status of your device.

✔ **System Updates:** Tap this (see Figure 3-13) to get information about your current operating system version and to manually check for and download system updates.

✔ **Language:** An obvious option, tapping this lets you choose the language you'd like Kindle Fire HDX to use onscreen from a list.

✔ **Text-to-Speech:** The Text-to-Speech feature allows your Kindle Fire to speak text that's displayed onscreen. Use this setting to download additional voices, including voices speaking in foreign languages, and select what type of voice you'd like Text-to-Speech to use.

✔ **Date & Time:** Your Kindle Fire HDX uses the Date & Time setting to display the correct time in the Status bar, and also to work with other apps, such as a third-party calendar app. Tap Date & Time to see the four options shown in Figure 3-14:

Figure 3-13: Amazon occasionally provides system updates; you can check for updates manually.

- *Time:* This setting is controlled by which time zone you select.

- *Date:* This setting is also controlled by which time zone you select.

- *Select Time Zone:* Tap the arrow to the right of this setting to change your time zone; next, tap to the right side of the time zone you want to use (see Figure 3-15).

- *Use 24-Hour Format:* If you want to use a 24-hour military-style clock, leave this setting on; if you'd rather use a 12-hour clock, tap to turn this setting off.

✔ **Storage:** Tells you how much memory is still available on your device.

✔ **Enable ADB:** With this setting on, people who develop apps for Kindle Fire HDX are allowed to debug their apps on HDX devices.

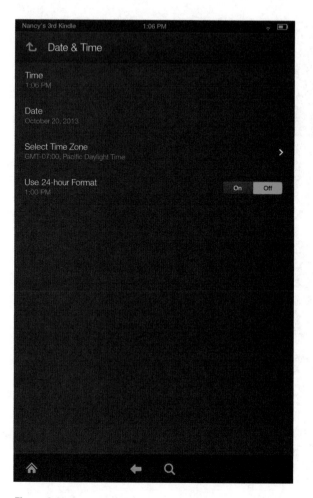

Figure 3-14: Get your HDX current by setting the correct date and time.

- ✔ **Serial Number:** You guessed it: Your device's serial number is displayed here.

- ✔ **Reset to Factory Defaults:** This setting could come in handy in a couple of situations. If you sell your Kindle Fire HDX to somebody (so that you can buy a newer version, of course!), you won't want that person to have your docs and contact information, so you can reset to get rid of this information.

Also, if you've loaded a lot of content onto your Kindle Fire HDX and then decide you want a clean beginning to clear up memory, you might choose to reset the device. If your HDX begins experiencing problems, resetting might get rid of what's causing those problems.

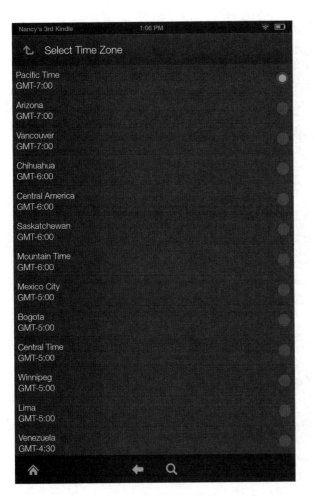

Figure 3-15: Manually set the time zone on your Kindle Fire HDX.

Resetting wipes all content and any changes you've made to default settings.

If you tap this setting, you see the confirming dialog box shown in Figure 3-16. Tap Erase Everything to continue with the reset procedure or Cancel to close the warning dialog box and halt the reset.

Although you get a minimum of 16GB of storage with Kindle Fire HDX, a chunk of that is taken up in pre-installed and system files. So the storage available may indicate that you have less total storage available on the device than you thought.

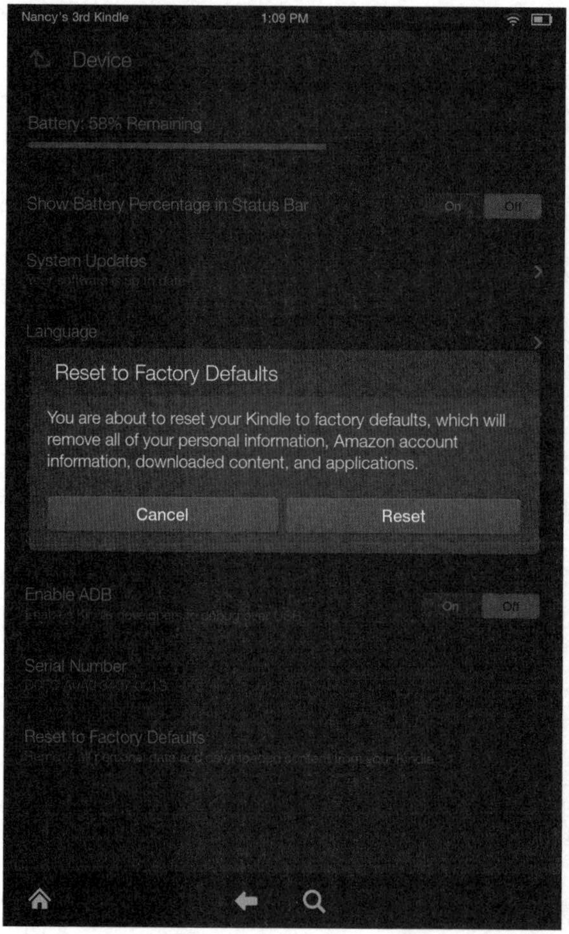

Figure 3-16: Be cautious when using the Reset feature.

Setting up Wireless and Networks

Wireless is a pretty essential setting for using Kindle Fire HDX. Without a Wi-Fi connection, you can't stream video or music, shop at the various Amazon stores, or send and receive e-mail.

Tap Wireless in the Settings screen to view the settings shown in Figure 3-17:

- ✔ **Airplane Mode:** Turn this setting on or off. With Airplane Mode on, you can't join a network.

- ✔ **Wi-Fi:** Tap Wi-Fi to go to more settings where you can turn the feature on or off. Note that turning Wi-Fi off may save some of your Kindle Fire HDX's battery life. With Wi-Fi on, you can tap a network on the list of available networks that appears to connect to it.

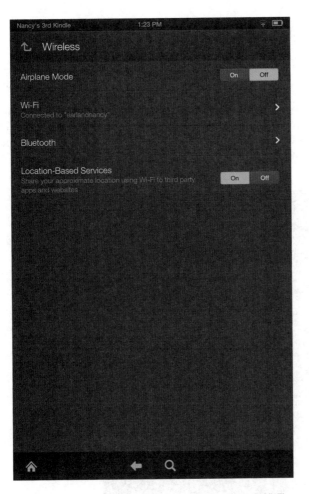

Figure 3-17: Turn on Wi-Fi and choose your preferred Wi-Fi network.

- ✔ **Bluetooth:** Tap here to access Bluetooth settings that allow you to enable and connect to a Bluetooth device such as a Bluetooth printer or cellphone.
- ✔ **Location-Based Services:** Tap to turn this feature on or off, depending on whether you want services such as a Maps app to ascertain your physical location.

Working with applications

Apps can help you do everything from manage e-mail to play games. Managing the way apps work on your Kindle Fire HDX is done through the Applications setting.

You access the Applications setting by tapping Applications on the Settings screen. The Applications screen (see Figure 3-18) provides you with a list of installed apps.

Tap any pre-installed app to choose settings for its particular options.

Tap Manage All Applications to see a list of all installed apps. When you tap one of these, you are presented with a Force Stop button that is useful if the app freezes, as well as information about the amount of memory the app and its data are taking up on your Kindle Fire.

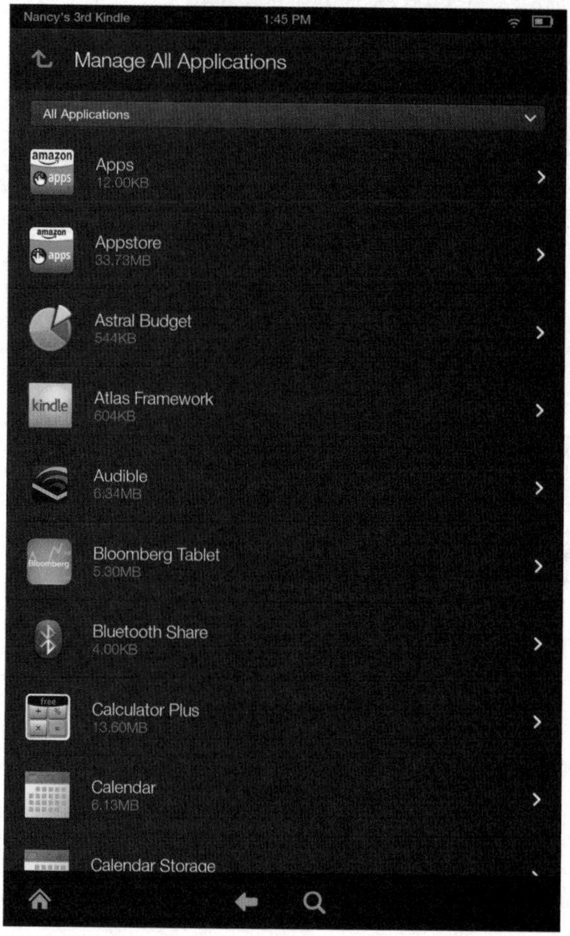

Figure 3-18: Each application on your Kindle Fire HDX has associated settings.

Choosing Settings for Notifications and Quiet Time

The settings for these features are all about how your Kindle Fire HDX lets you know about an event, such as a completed download or an incoming message.

You can use the Quiet Time settings to turn Quiet Time on or off, or set up a schedule of quiet times, for example every day when it's baby's nap time or your yoga retreat. Tap the Quiet Time button to turn audible alerts off, and tap it again to turn them on.

To set up a scheduled Quiet Time, follow these steps:

1. **Swipe down to display the Quick Settings bar.**
2. **Tap Settings.**
3. **Tap Notifications & Quiet Time.**
4. **Tap the Scheduled Quiet Time button to turn this feature on.**
5. **Tap any of the options to turn on Quiet Time when you are, for example, listening to Audiobooks or MP3s or Browsing in Silk.**
6. **Tap the Schedule option at the bottom of the page to turn it on; you can then scroll the time setting in the From and To sections to schedule a regular quiet time each day of a preset interval, such as from 10:00 to 11:00 am each morning.**

There's also a list of apps that you can tap to select how those apps can notify you. Notifications can be shown in the Notification tray that appears when you swipe down from the top of the screen, or they can play a sound.

Controlling display and sounds

With a tablet that's so media-centric, accessing music and video, as well as games that you can play with their accompanying screeches and sounds, it's important that you know how to control the volume.

If you tap Display & Sounds in Settings (see Figure 3-19), you see a volume slider that you can use to increase or decrease the volume, as well as a slider that you can move to dim or enhance the screen's brightness (dimmer to the left, brighter to the right).

Notifications may come from the arrival of a new e-mail or a completed download, or an app might notify you of something (such as an appointment reminder from a calendar app that you may have downloaded). The Notification Sound setting allows you to select what Notification sounds you will hear from a list of cute sound names like Deneb or Fleuron, which tell you just about nothing about what the sound will sound like. When you tap a sound name, however, you hear a preview sound of it to help you make your choice.

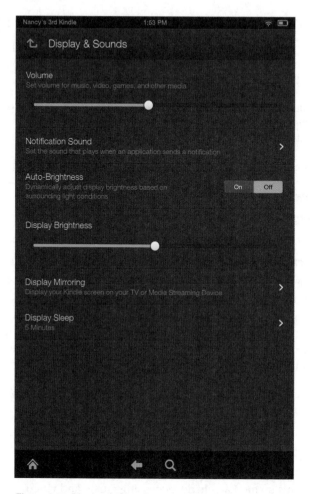

Figure 3-19: Display & Sounds settings are pretty darn simple to use.

Display & Sounds also allows you to manage your device's display, adjusting both the screen brightness and turning on Auto-Brightness, a feature that adjusts the screen light for optimal viewing in different lighting settings.

 ✓ **Display Mirroring**: If you want to have your Kindle Fire HDX screen appear on your TV or a monitor, tap this setting to select a device that you can make discoverable (much as you make a cellphone discoverable to your car's Bluetooth setup). This setting is great for playing games on your Kindle Fire while viewing it on a larger screen.

 ✓ **Display Sleep:** After a certain period of inactivity, the Kindle Fire HDX screen will lock and go black to save battery power. You can adjust the length of this interval by tapping the arrow in this field and choosing from a list of time intervals that ranges from 30 seconds to one hour. You can also choose the option Never if you want your screen to be always on. However, remember that using the Never option will wear down your battery more quickly.

Working with the onscreen keyboard

Your Kindle Fire HDX has no physical keyboard, so you depend on its onscreen keyboard to provide input to apps such as OfficeSuite, or in fields used to search and enter text into forms, such as e-mail messages.

There are three simple things you can do when you choose Keyboards from the Settings list: set the Language, manage Keyboard settings, and manage the Bluetooth Keyboard settings (see Figure 3-20). Tapping Language allows you to choose the language for your keyboard. Tapping Bluetooth Keyboard lets you choose the language for a keyboard that appears when using a Bluetooth connection. Tapping Keyboard Settings displays these options:

- **Sound on Keypress:** If you like that satisfying clicky sound when you tap a key on the onscreen keyboard, tap to turn this setting on.

- **Auto Correction:** Turning this setting on and choosing a correction level (such as Modest or Very Aggressive) allows Kindle Fire HDX to correct common typing errors, such as typing *teh* when you mean *the*.

- **Auto-Capitalization:** If you want Kindle Fire HDX to automatically capitalize proper names or the first word in a sentence, tap to turn this setting on.

- **Next Word Prediction:** Tap this option and Kindle Fire HDX will show word suggestions as you type to speed up your text entry.

- **Check Spelling:** If you turn this feature on, words in text fields that might be misspelled are highlighted.

- **Personal Dictionary**: An English dictionary is included with Kindle Fire HDX out of the box. If you download or sideload other dictionaries, they will be listed when you tap this button, and you can select from the list of dictionaries the one you want the keyboard to use for features such as word prediction and spell checking.

New and Improved Accessibility Features

If you have challenges with manual dexterity (for example, carpal tunnel syndrome or arthritis), vision, or hearing, you may find that Accessibility features can help you in using your Kindle Fire HDX.

Here's a quick rundown of available accessibility features:

- **Screen Reader:** Screen Reader audibly describes the actions you're taking on your Kindle Fire HDX. If you turn this setting on, the Reading

Speed and Explore by Touch settings become available. Turning Screen Reader on also turns on Explore by Touch. The way you interact with your Kindle Fire changes dramatically when you turn these features on, so I strongly suggest you walk through the tutorial that's offered before you start to work with them. The most important thing to know is that when turned on, you have to tap and then double-tap items onscreen to perform an action.

✔ **Explore by Touch:** With this setting on, you can use gestures to interact with items on the device. There are five accessibility shortcut gestures that you can use to go home, go back, or gain access to notifications, the menu for an active app, and Kindle Fire HDX's accessibility settings. When you turn this feature on, an Explore by Touch tutorial appears and walks you through how to use the feature.

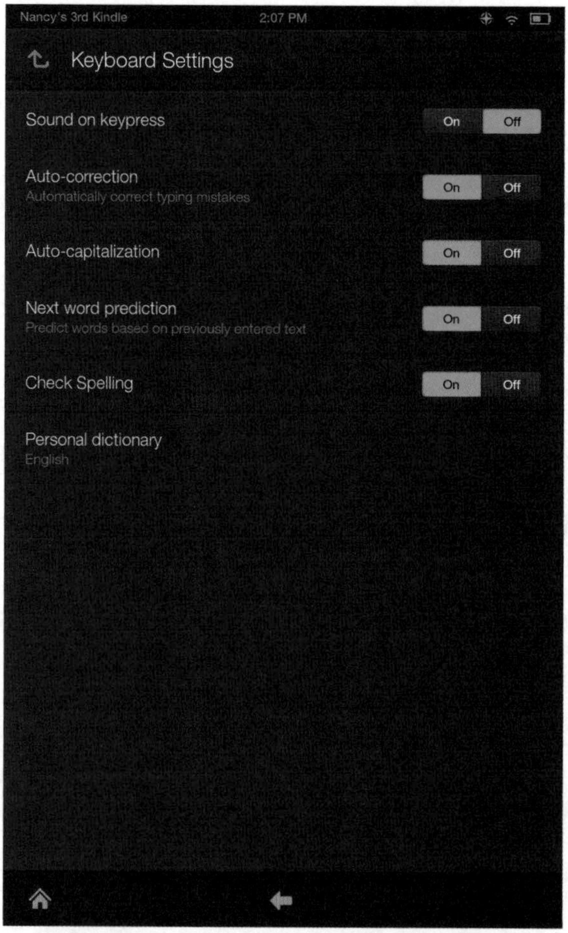

Figure 3-20: Control your onscreen keyboard with these settings.

✔ **Screen Magnifier:** Toggles on and off a feature that enlarges your entire screen. Once turned on, triple-tapping magnifies the screen, and you can then control the screen magnification by pinching your fingers inward or outward. Also, with Screen Magnifier on and the page enlarged, swiping two fingers across the screen allows you to move around the page to see portions of it that may now be off screen.

✔ **Use Large Font Size:** Toggles on and off larger fonts onscreen.

✔ **Closed Captioning:** Turns on closed captioning for videos; note that only some videos are enabled for closed captioning.

✔ **Convert Stereo to Mono:** If you have poor hearing in one ear, stereo sound can make you miss some of the audio coming at you. You can use this setting to turn on Mono audio.

✔ **Accessibility User's Guide:** For a quick tutorial on how to use various accessibility features, tap this and scroll through the user's guide that's displayed.

✔ **Explore by Touch Tutorial:** Tap this setting to bring up the Explore by Touch tutorial, which also appears automatically when you turn on the Explore by Touch feature.

Making security settings

The first thing you can do to keep your Kindle Fire HDX secure is to never let it out of your hands. But because we can't control everything and sometimes things get lost or stolen, it's a good idea to assign a password that's required to unlock your Kindle Fire HDX screen. If other people then get their hands on your Kindle Fire HDX, they have no way to get at stored data, such as your Amazon account information or contacts, without knowing the password.

In Settings, tap the Security option and you'll see three choices (see Figure 3-21):

✔ **Lock Screen Password:** Simply tap the On button to require that a PIN be used to unlock your device. When you do, fields appear labeled New PIN and Confirm New PIN. Think of a PIN, fill the fields in, and tap Finish to save your new PIN.

✔ **Credential Storage:** Credentials are typically used for Microsoft Exchange–based accounts, such as an account you use to access e-mail on your company's server. If you use Microsoft Exchange, it's a good idea to get your network administrator's help to make the following settings: Install Secure Credentials, Trusted Credentials, and Clear Credential Storage.

✔ **Device Administrators:** If your device is being administered through a company Exchange account, use this setting to establish the device administrator who can modify settings for the account.

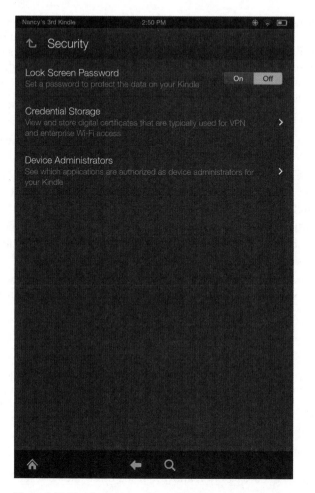

Figure 3-21: The Security settings offer three ways to secure your Kindle Fire HDX.

Part II
Taking the Leap Online

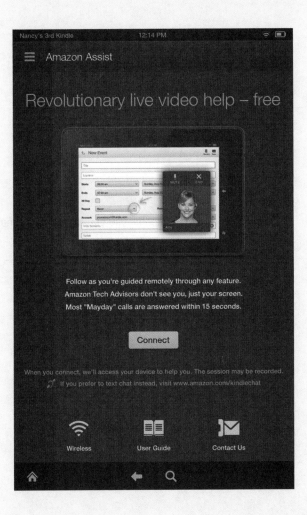

Visit www.dummies.com/extras/kindlefirehdx for advice about staying safe while going online with your Kindle Fire HDX.

In this part...

- ✔ Go shopping for apps, music, video and more.
- ✔ Discover how to use the Silk browser.
- ✔ Set up your e-mail account so that you can access your Inbox from Kindle Fire HDX.

4

Going Shopping

In This Chapter

▶ Using your Amazon account

▶ Shopping at the Amazon Appstore

▶ Buying apps, music, video, and printed publications

▶ Buying other Amazon items through your Kindle Fire HDX

*B*ecause Kindle Fire HDX is, above all, a great device for consuming content (especially Amazon-provided content), knowing how to buy that content or download free content is key to enjoying it. Amazon offers a rich supply of books, magazines, music, and video as well as an Appstore that you can use to get your hands on apps that add to the functionality of your Kindle Fire HDX. These apps can range from simple accessories such as a notes program to fun and addictive games and maps programs.

In this chapter, you discover how to get apps as well as books, magazines, music, audiobooks, and videos for your Kindle Fire HDX.

Managing Your Amazon Account

You buy things from Amazon by using the account and payment information you provide when you create an Amazon account. You probably have an account if you have ever bought anything on Amazon (or opened an account when you bought your Kindle Fire HDX). If you haven't opened an account, you should go to www.amazon.com, and when you attempt to purchase something, you'll be asked for your Amazon credentials. Tap the No, I Am A New Customer option and follow the steps to obtain your account credentials.

To buy things on Amazon with your Kindle Fire HDX, you need to have associated your Amazon account with your Kindle Fire HDX, which happens during the setup process, covered in Chapter 2. You can change the account to which your Kindle Fire is registered by deregistering it and then registering it to the Amazon credentials for the other account. For example, if you prefer to have purchases charged to your spouse's Amazon account or you are giving your Kindle Fire to somebody else, you might want to associate it with a different Amazon account. You can do this by following these steps:

1. **Swipe down from the top of the screen to display Quick Settings.**

2. **Tap Settings.**

3. **Tap My Account (see Figure 4-1).**

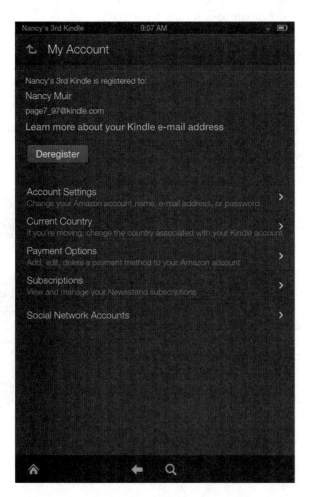

Figure 4-1: Choose account settings on this screen.

4. **Tap the Deregister button.**

5. **A confirming screen appears.**

6. **Tap Deregister.**

7. **Tap the Register button.**

8. **Enter your preferred Amazon credentials (e-mail address and a password) for the account you want to associate with your device.**

9. **Tap Create Account.**

After you associate your device with an Amazon account, you can manage account settings and payment options by following these steps:

1. **Navigate to the Amazon website (**`www.amazon.com`**) by using the browser on either your Kindle Fire HDX or your computer.**

2. **Tap (if you're using a touchscreen device) or click the Your Account option in the top-right corner of the Amazon screen (see Figure 4-2).**

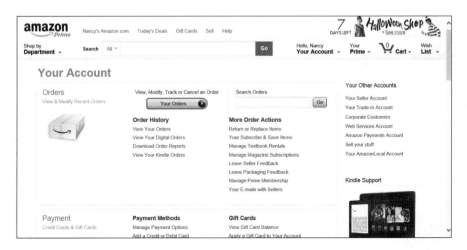

Figure 4-2: Managing your Amazon account on a PC.

3. **Tap or click the Manage Payment Options or Add a Credit or Debit Card option from the Payment section of your account.**

4. **Change or enter a new method of payment and billing address using the Delete or Edit buttons.**

Your changes are automatically saved. Now when you purchase items from your Amazon Kindle Fire HDX, those payment and billing options are used to complete the purchase.

Visiting the Amazon Appstore

After you register your Amazon account with your Kindle Fire HDX (which I discuss in the preceding section), you can start shopping for all kinds of content for your Kindle Fire HDX. I'll start by introducing you to the world of apps.

Apps provide you with functionality of all kinds, from an app that turns your Kindle Fire HDX into a star-gazing instrument to game apps. You can find acupuncture apps, drawing apps, and apps that provide maps so that you can find your way in the world.

Exploring the world of apps

You can buy apps for your Kindle Fire HDX by using the Amazon Appstore. This store is full of apps written especially for devices that are based on the Android platform, including Kindle Fire HDX.

Android devices may have slightly different operating systems, and therefore not every app will work on every device. See Chapters 11 and 12 for some suggested apps that will work well with your Kindle Fire HDX.

Follow these steps to explore the world of apps:

1. **Tap the Apps button at the top of the Home screen to enter your Apps library.**

2. **Tap the Store button.**

   The Appstore appears (see Figure 4-3).

3. **(Optional) At the top of the Appstore is Today's Free App of the Day; tap this option to download a free app to your device.**

You can get a different free app every day; just be sure you don't glut your Kindle Fire HDX's memory with free apps you're not really going to use.

Swipe upward to scroll down the page to view recommendations for you in categories such as Games or Finance (see Figure 4-4). You can also swipe to the right to reveal more apps in each category. Tap the Left Nav button in the top-left corner to display the Navigation panel. From here you can select categories of apps such as Games (see Figure 4-5), Best Sellers, and New Releases.

Tap Browse Categories in the Navigation panel to see a list of all categories of apps such as Entertainment and Cooking; then tap on a category to go there.

Figure 4-3: The Amazon Appstore.

Searching for apps

You can have fun browsing through categories of apps, but if you know which app you want to buy, using the Search feature can take you right to it.

To search for an app, follow these steps:

1. **Tap in the Search field on the Appstore's main page.**

   The keyboard shown in Figure 4-6 appears.

2. **Using the onscreen keyboard, enter the name of an app, such as Angry Birds.**

   Suggested matches to the search term appear beneath the Search field.

3. **Tap a suggested search term to display a list of detailed results, as shown in Figure 4-7.**

4. **Tap an app name in the results to see an app description page.**

   The Product Info screen appears, as shown in Figure 4-8. Read the description and scroll down to read customer reviews or explore other apps that customers who bought this app also bought.

Figure 4-4: Get recommendations of great games you might enjoy.

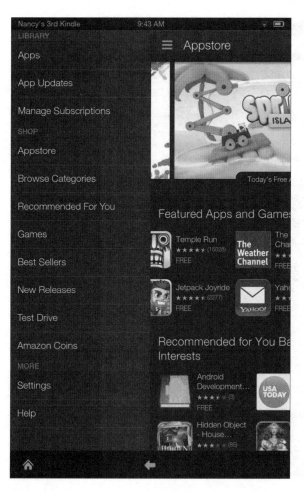

Figure 4-5: See categories of apps by using the Navigation panel.

Buying apps

You can use your Amazon account payment option to buy apps, or you can use Amazon Coins, a new feature that lets you buy apps and games with pre-paid credits. When you use Coins, you can get savings in prices — as much as 10 percent. When you buy a new Kindle Fire HDX, it comes with 500 coins, which is about $5 in real money. I tell you more about using the coins in the upcoming steps.

Whether you find something you want to own by browsing or searching, when you're ready to buy, follow these steps:

Figure 4-6: Use the Search field and onscreen keyboard in the Appstore to find what you want.

1. **From the app's Product Info screen (see the preceding section), tap the Price button.**

   Note that if the app is free, this button reads Free, but if you have to pay for the app, the app price (such as $0.99) and the number of corresponding coins is displayed on the button. When you tap the button for a paid item, the dialog box shown in Figure 4-9 appears.

2. **Tap the Get App button to download paid or free apps to your Kindle Fire HDX.**

   A Downloading button appears, showing the download progress. When the installation is complete, an Open button appears.

3. **If you want to use the app immediately, tap the Open button.**

   To use the app at any time, locate it in the App library or, if you've used it recently, on the Carousel; tap the app to open it. Each app has its own controls and settings, so look for a Settings menu like the one for the Solitaire game shown in Figure 4-10.

You can also buy apps from the Appstore on your PC or Mac. When placing the app in your shopping cart, be sure to select Kindle Fire HDX for the device you want to download the app to in the drop-down list below the Add to Cart button. When you complete your purchase, assuming that you're in range of a Wi-Fi network, the app is immediately downloaded to your Kindle Fire HDX.

Figure 4-7: Search results in the Appstore.

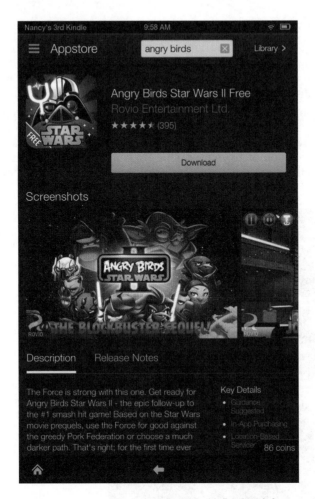

Figure 4-8: Product details are shown in the Product Info screen.

To delete an installed app from your App library, press and hold it until a menu appears and then tap Remove from Device. The app, however, isn't gone — it's still stored in the Amazon Cloud Drive, and you can download it again at any time by tapping it when you're in the Cloud tab of the App library.

Buying Content

Apps and games are great, but shopping for content is my favorite thing to do. I'm not putting down games and map apps, but to me, content means a night at the movies, a rainy afternoon with a good book, or a relaxing hour listening to a soothing collection of music.

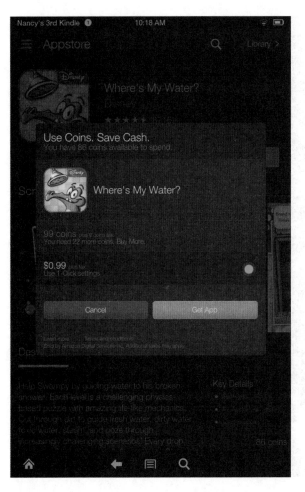

Figure 4-9: Tap Buy App or Get App to make the app your own.

From Amazon, you can buy publications, books, music, audiobooks, and video (movies and TV shows) to download or stream to your Kindle Fire HDX. The buying process is somewhat similar for the different types of content, but there are slight variations, which I go into in the following sections.

Buying publictions through Newsstand

There's a world of periodicals out there, from magazines to newspapers, just waiting for you to explore them. Kindle Fire HDX's color display makes browsing through color magazines especially appealing.

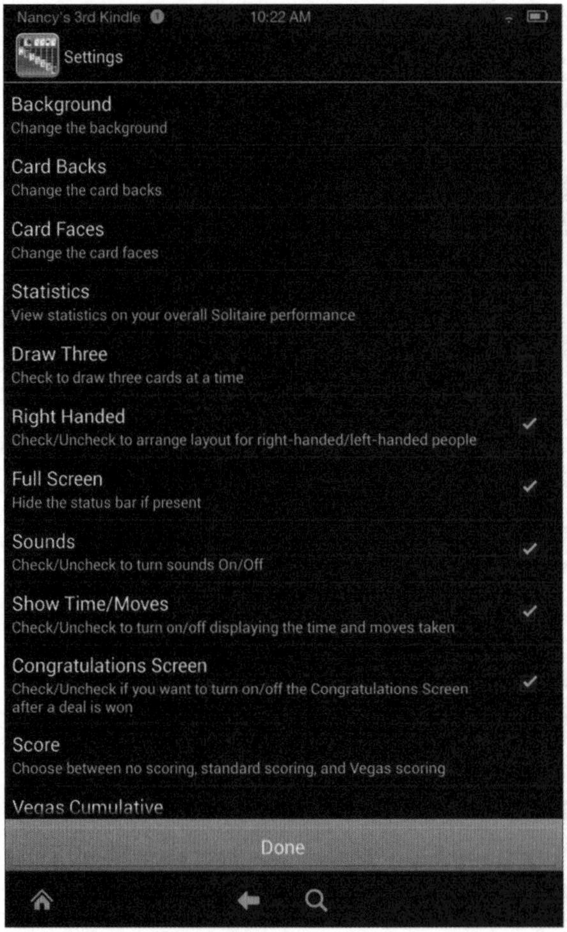

Figure 4-10: App settings for Solitaire.

Tap Newsstand on the Home page of Kindle Fire HDX and then tap the Store button to see several categories of items (see Figure 4-11).

First, there are the Kindle Magazine of the Month and Most Popular Magazines. Featured Deals on Kindle Magazines is a category where you'll find deals such as 30-day free trials. You can swipe right to left to scroll through each category.

Below, you see categories such as Magazines for Her, Featured Newspapers, and Recipes (though the categories might change on a regular basis). You can tap the See More button above any category to see a more complete list of included items.

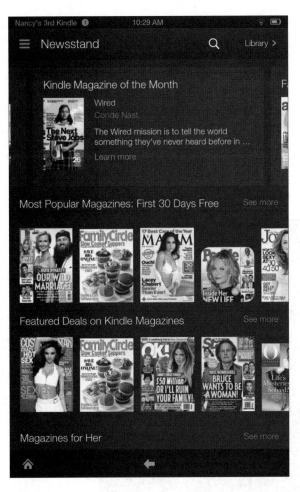

Figure 4-11: The Newsstand store.

When you find the publication you want, follow these steps to buy or subscribe to it:

1. **Tap the item.**

   A screen appears showing pricing, a description of the publication, and Subscribe Now and Buy Issue buttons (see Figure 4-12).

2. **Tap Subscribe Now or Buy Issue.**

   The button label changes to read Downloading. During the download process, you can tap the Cancel button if you change your mind. When the download is complete, the button label changes to Read Now.

3. **Tap the Read Now button to open the magazine.**

Note that the magazine is stored in your Amazon Cloud library, where you can read or download it to your Kindle Fire HDX via Newsstand at a later time.

Buying books

I may be partial to books because I write them, but I hardly think I'm alone. If you've joined the electronic book revolution (or even if you haven't), you'll find that reading books on Kindle Fire HDX is convenient and economical (e-books are typically a few dollars less than the print version, and you can borrow e-books from your local library for free).

Figure 4-12: Details about a publication and buttons to help you purchase or subscribe.

To browse through e-books from Amazon on your Kindle Fire HDX, follow these steps:

1. **Tap the Books button on the Kindle Fire HDX Home screen.**

2. **Tap the Store button.**

   The Amazon Bookstore sports a Recommended for You section near the top that suggests books for you based on your buying history.

3. **Swipe right to left to scroll through the recommendations.**

   You also see categories such as Kindle Select 25, New & Noteworthy, and Monthly Deals.

As with the Newsstand, when you locate and tap an item in the bookstore, you see a screen with that item's pricing and description (see Figure 4-13). In the bookstore, the buttons you see at this point are labeled Download Sample, Buy (or Buy for Free), and More Options. Here's how these three buttons work:

- **Download a Sample:** Tap this button, and it changes to a Downloading button and then to a Read Now button. Tap the Read Now button to open the sample of the book.

- **Buy or Buy for Free:** Tap this button, and it changes to a Downloading button. When the download is complete, the button label changes to Read Now. Tap the Read Now button to open the book. Remember that the book is now stored in your Books library, where you can tap it to open and read it at your leisure.

- **More Options:** This button offers two options, Add to Wish List and Print Edition From, with the price showing on the right of the button. Tap Add to Wish List so that you can easily find it again in the Navigation panel of the store to buy it at a later date. Tap Print Editions From to add the item to your Amazon shopping cart and specify shipping information.

The sample or purchased book appears in your Books library, which you reach by tapping Books from the Home screen and then tapping the Library tab. After you've read a bit of your new book, it will appear both in your Books library and on the Carousel on the Home screen.

To remove a book from your device (remembering that it will still be stored in the Amazon Cloud), open your Books library, press and hold the book image, and tap Remove from Device from the menu that appears.

For more about reading e-books and periodicals on Kindle Fire HDX, see Chapter 6.

Figure 4-13: Details about a book in the Amazon Bookstore.

Buying music

You may hate computer games, and you might not read books very often, but I've never met anybody who doesn't like some kind of music. No matter what kind of music you prefer, from hip-hop to Broadway, you're likely to find a great many selections tucked away in Amazon's vaults.

Tap the Music button on the Kindle Fire HDX Home screen and then tap the Store button. Near the middle of the screen, you'll see Songs Recommended for You (see Figure 4-14). These are based on music you've previously purchased. You can also tap categories such as Top New Albums and Top New Songs to view music by these criteria.

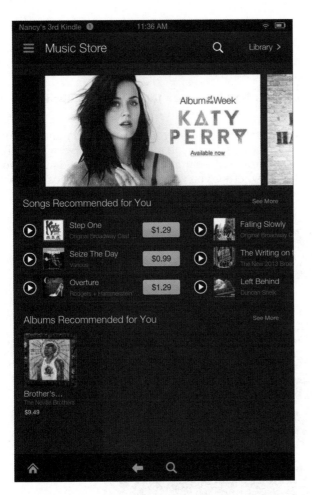

Figure 4-14: The Amazon Music store.

All over the Music store Home page, you'll see thumbnails of music selections.

Follow these steps to buy music:

1. **Tap an item.**

   A screen appears, displaying a list of the songs in the case of an album with Price buttons for both the entire album and each individual song.

2. **Tap the arrow button to the left of a song to play a preview of it.**

3. **Tap a Buy Album For button, with the price of the album also displayed on the button.**

   The button label changes from the price of the item to the word Buy.

4. **Tap the Buy button.**

   The song or album downloads to your Music library. A confirmation screen appears, displaying a Play Now button and a Continue Shopping button (see Figure 4-15).

5. **Tap the Play Now button to open the album and display the list of songs.**

   The album is now stored both in your Music library and the Amazon Cloud. If you tap a song to play it, it'll also appear with recently accessed content in the Carousel. The first time you download music, you may be asked to choose whether you want content automatically downloaded to your device when you buy it.

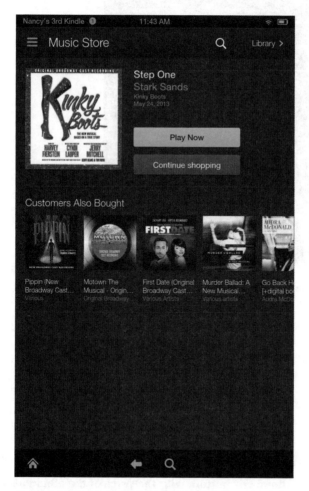

Figure 4-15: This dialog box allows you to return to your library or keep shopping.

If you tap the Continue Shopping button, you can later find the album in your Music library.

See Chapter 7 for more about playing music.

Buying video

You should definitely check out the experience of consuming your video programs on a portable device such as Kindle Fire HDX. From lying in bed or on the beach to watching your videos while waiting in line at the bank, portability can be a very convenient feature.

When you tap Videos on the Kindle Fire HDX Home screen, you're instantly taken to the Amazon Video store, shown in Figure 4-16.

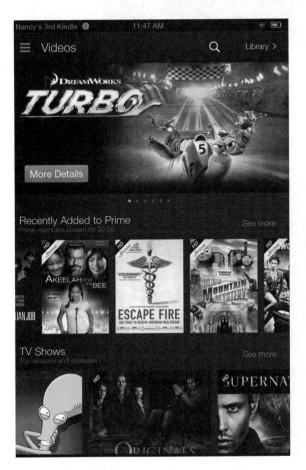

Figure 4-16: Shop for video in the Amazon Video store.

Across the middle of the screen, you see thumbnails of items recently added to the Prime Instant Videos category. You can also scroll down to view shows that offer a First Episode Free so that you can sample shows that are new to you.

Tap an item in any category, and a descriptive screen appears. For TV shows, this screen includes episode prices for TV shows and a set of Season tabs. For movies, this screen may include Watch Trailer, Buy, and Rent buttons (see Figure 4-17). You can also scroll down and view details about the movie's director, release year, and more.

Tap a Price button, and the button becomes a Rent or Buy button. Tap this button, and your purchase or rental is processed.

Figure 4-17: The video screen offers several options.

Tap a Rent button for movies, and you see a green button labeled Rent with the price displayed. Tap this, and you're immediately charged for the rental. The rental period begins when you start to watch the movie.

See Chapter 8 for more about playing videos.

If you tap the Add to Watchlist button, the item is added to your Watchlist so that you can go back and rent or buy it at some future time. To view your Watchlist, tap the Left Nav button when in the Videos library or store and then tap Your Watchlist. Tap any item to open a screen similar to the one shown in Figure 4-17.

Shopping for Anything Else

Amazon kindly pre-installed an Amazon Shopping app on your Kindle Fire HDX so that you can quickly go to their online store and buy anything your heart desires.

The Amazon Shopping app (see Figure 4-18) is included Kindle Fire HDX right out of the box. Just tap Shop from the Kindle Fire HDX Home screen and then tap Shop Amazon. Amazon opens in your browser with a list of recommendations for you, based on previous purchases. You can tap the Shop by Departments tab to access a drop-down list of available departments.

Now, proceed to shop as you usually do on Amazon, tapping any item of interest to add it to your cart and using your Amazon account information to pay and arrange for shipping.

Figure 4-18: Tap the Shop Amazon app to go shopping for virtually anything.

5

Going Online

In This Chapter

▶ Using Wi-Fi on your Kindle Fire HDX

▶ Browsing the web with Silk

▶ Personalizing Silk's settings

▶ Managing Privacy settings

▶ Setting up e-mail

*Y*ears ago, the best way to stay in touch with the outside world was by reading the morning paper and going to the mailbox to get your mail. Today, browsing the web and checking e-mail has replaced this routine in many of our lives. Kindle Fire HDX can become your new go-to device for keeping informed and in touch by using Amazon's Silk browser and the pre-installed e-mail client.

In this chapter, you discover the ins and outs of browsing with Silk and the simple tools you can use to send and receive e-mail on Kindle Fire HDX.

Getting Online by Using Wi-Fi

Unless you own a 4G LTE version of Kindle Fire HDX, Kindle Fire HDX is a Wi-Fi–only device, meaning that you have to connect to a nearby Wi-Fi network to go online. You might access a Wi-Fi connection through your home network, at work, or via a public hotspot, such as an Internet cafe or airport.

When you first set up your Kindle Fire HDX (as described in Chapter 2), you can choose a Wi-Fi network to use for going online. If you want to log on to a different network, follow these steps:

1. **Swipe down from the top of the Home screen to display Quick Settings, which reveals a menu of common settings, such as Quiet Time, Wireless, and Brightness.**

2. **Tap Wireless.**

   Wireless settings appear (see Figure 5-1).

3. **Tap Wi-Fi.**

4. **Tap a network in the list of available wireless networks to sign in.**

   You have to enter a password to sign in to some networks. If you're already connected to a network when you tap it here, you get information about the connection (the signal strength, link speed, and so on).

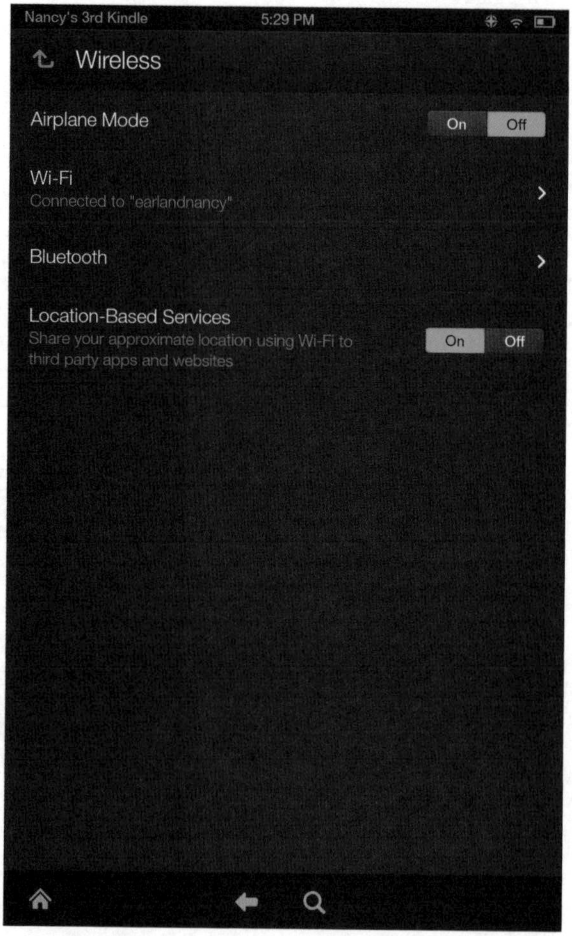

Figure 5-1: Wireless settings allow you to select an available network to join.

Browsing the Internet with Silk

Silk is a browser created by Amazon. Some people wondered why Amazon didn't choose to use an existing browser, such as Internet Explorer, for Kindle Fire HDX. The answer is that Silk takes advantage of Amazon's ability to use its own servers to make your browsing experience fast.

For example, if you visit a popular news website and choose to tap the headline story to get more details, the odds are that many thousands of people have done the same thing. The Silk browser recognizes this pattern and holds that next page in its *cache* (a dedicated block of memory) to deliver it quickly to you if you also make this selection. This ability is supposed to make your browsing experience as fast and smooth as, well, silk.

The latest version of Silk offers a few new features and speedier browsing. Reading View allows you to view content without the typical distracting web page chaos. A new panel that slides out on the left of the screen offers shortcuts such as Most Visited and Bookmarked sites. These selections make it simpler to find pages in a neat grid pattern of thumbnails.

In the following sections, I introduce you to Silk's browser environment. Many tools and features will be familiar to you from other browsers, but a few are unique to Silk.

Using navigation tools to get around

From the Kindle Fire HDX's Home screen, you can tap the Web button to display the Silk browser. You can also reach Silk by tapping its thumbnail in the grid at the bottom of your Home screen.

Items in the Options bar help you to navigate among web pages, as shown in Figure 5-2. You can do the following:

- Use the Back and Forward buttons on the Options bar to move among pages you've previously viewed.

- To search for a page, tap the Search button, enter a site address or search term using the onscreen keyboard, and then tap Enter. Results of the search are displayed.

- Tap the Full Screen button (it looks like four arrows pointing outward) to remove the address bar from the screen for easier reading.

- Tap the Menu button to add a bookmark, search on the page, or share the page with others via Email, Facebook, Twitter, or Skype (more about these features in later sections of this chapter). Note that if you're on a page that is already bookmarked, the item in the menu reads Edit Bookmark.

Figure 5-2: Silk offers a familiar browser interface.

Displaying tabs

Silk uses tabs that allow you to display more than one web page at a time and move among those pages. Follow these steps to add a tab:

1. **Tap the Add button in the top-right corner — which features a plus sign (+) — to add a tab in the browser.**

   A list of most visited sites appears.

2. **Tap a thumbnail, or you can tap in the Search/Address bar that appears when you add a tab and enter a URL by using the onscreen keyboard; then tap Go on the keyboard.**

   You are taken to that site.

Turning on Reading View

When you're in a view that contains content such as an article, you can turn on the new Reading View to remove clutter from the screen and focus on the text. Reading View hides both the address bar and ads, as well as most images from the article.

To turn Reading View on:

1. **Navigate to a page with an article on it.**

   For example, Amazon.com is a site that won't offer Reading View but CNN.com, a news site, will.

2. **Locate the article you want to read and tap somewhere within it.**

3. **Tap the Reading View button to the right of the address bar.**

   The article text appears and web page clutter goes away (see Figure 5-3).

4. **Tap the Close button in the upper-right of the article to close Reading View.**

Bookmarking sites

You can bookmark sites in Silk so that you can easily jump back to them again. Here are the steps to add a Bookmark for a displayed page:

1. **With a site displayed onscreen, tap the Menu button in the Options bar (refer to Figure 5-2).**

   The menu shown in Figure 5-4 appears.

2. **Tap Add Bookmark.**

   The Add Bookmark dialog box appears.

3. **If you want, you can enter a new name in the Name field.**

4. **Tap OK.**

   The currently displayed page is bookmarked and the dialog box closes.

5. **Tap the Left Nav button on the top left of the screen to display the Silk panel.**

6. **Tap Bookmarks and then tap a bookmarked site's thumbnail (see Figure 5-5) to go there.**

 To delete a bookmark, after displaying thumbnails of bookmarked pages, press and hold a page. In the menu that appears, tap Delete. In the confirming dialog box that appears, tap OK and the bookmark is removed.

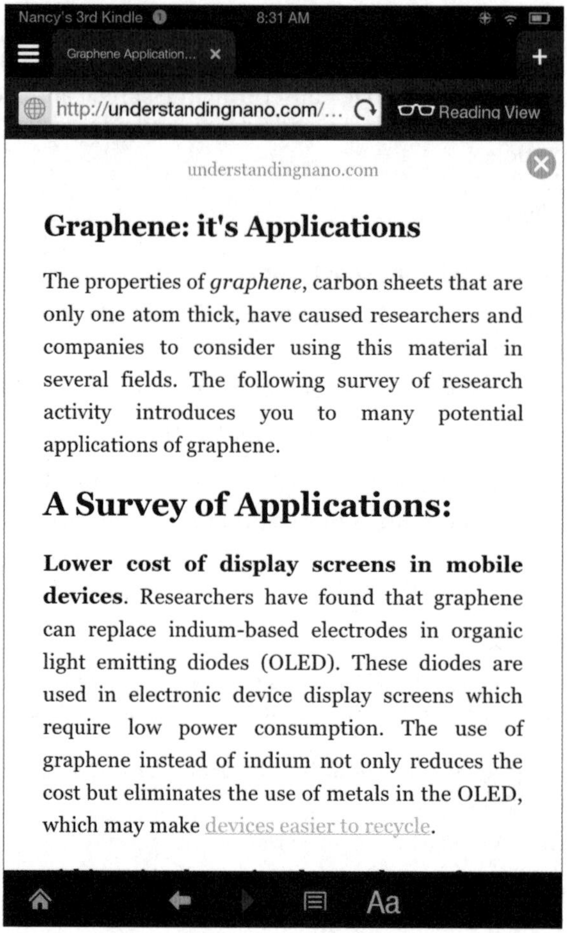

Figure 5-3: This cleaner view of your article is much easier to read.

Using Web content shortcuts

New with the latest version of Silk is a handy panel of shortcuts you can access from any page. In addition to Help and Settings for Silk, this panel, shown in Figure 5-6, provides shortcuts to

- Most Visited sites
- Bookmarks
- Downloads
- History of your browsing
- Trending Now news stories

Figure 5-4: Bookmarks help you quickly return to a favorite page.

To use this panel, follow these steps:

1. **Tap the Left Nav button in the top-left corner of the Silk screen.**

   The panel shown in Figure 5-6 appears.

2. **Tap an item, such as Trending Now.**

   Thumbnails of hot news stories with descriptive captions appear (see Figure 5-7).

Note that the results will vary slightly depending on what you select in Step 2. For example, History will display a list of items, whereas Bookmarks will display thumbnails of websites.

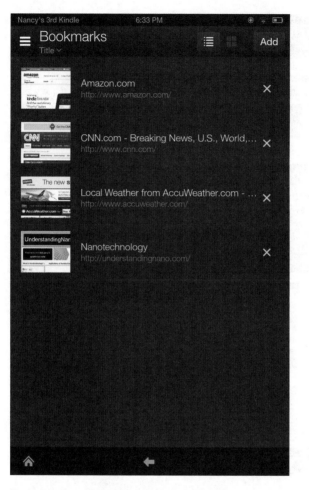

Figure 5-5: Choose your bookmarked site from this page.

Choosing Silk's General settings

At the bottom of the panel described in the previous section is a Settings button. When you tap that button, you can choose the following General settings (note that Saved Data settings are covered in the later section, "Choosing Privacy Settings"):

- **Search Engine:** Tap this setting to go to a dialog box where you can choose Bing, Google, or Yahoo! as your default search engine.

- **Block Pop-Up Windows:** Some sites generate pop-up windows, some of which are useful and many of which are just annoying ads. Tap this setting and select Ask, Never, or Always to control how and when pop-ups appear on web pages.

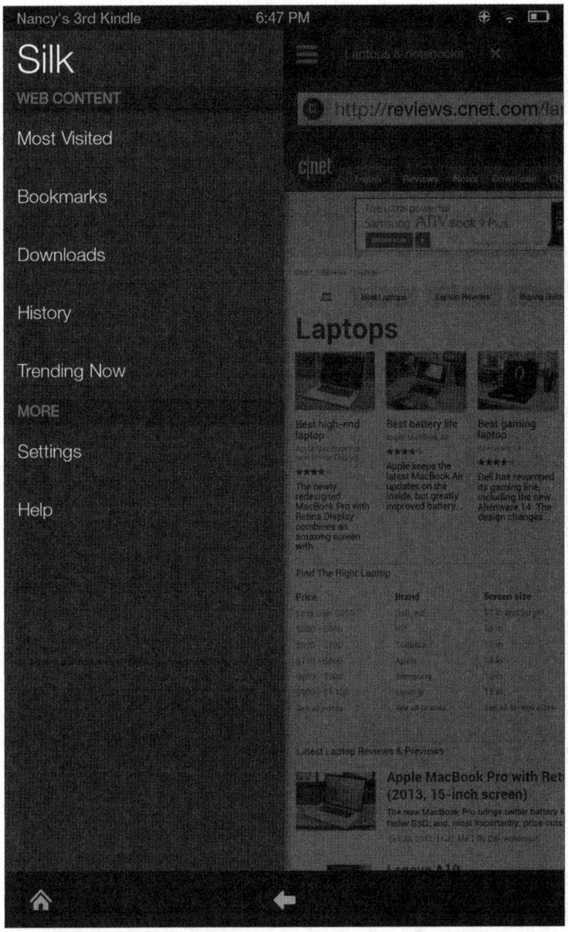

Figure 5-6: A new panel of shortcuts appears to the left.

- **Accelerate Page Loading:** Choosing this option allows Amazon to route requests through its servers in some situations so that your pages display more quickly.

- **Optional Encryption:** When you browse, requests for page content go through servers, either those used by the page owner or Amazon's servers. To protect this information, you can encrypt it by turning on Optional Encryption. Be aware, however, that turning this feature on may slow down your browsing experience slightly.

- **Enable Instant Page Loads:** If you turn off Accelerate Page Loading, this feature also turns off. You *can* leave Accelerate Page Loading on and turn this feature off, however. What this controls is whether Amazon can observe browsing behavior of the population and preload popular content, so if you choose to display it, it displays faster.

Figure 5-7: Trending news stories keep you up to date.

Searching for content on a page

Web pages can contain a lot of content, so it's not always easy to find the article or discussion you want to view on a particular topic. Most browsers provide a feature to search for content on a web page, and Silk is no exception.

To search the currently displayed page by using Silk, follow these steps:

1. **Tap Menu on the Options bar.**

2. **In the list of options that appears (see Figure 5-8), tap Find in Page.**

   The onscreen keyboard appears with the Search field active.

Figure 5-8: Search the currently displayed page.

3. **Type a search term.**

   The first instance of a match for the search term on the page appears in an orange highlight. Subsequent instances of the word on that page are highlighted in yellow, as shown in Figure 5-9.

4. **Tap any of these highlighted words to view the related content.**

5. **Tap Done to close the keyboard and end the search.**

Searching the web

Most of us spend a lot of our time online browsing around to find what we want. Search engines make our lives easier because they help us narrow down what we're looking for by using specific search terms; they then troll the web to find matches for those terms from a variety of sources.

Figure 5-9: The first instance of a word on a page is highlighted in orange.

To search the entire web, follow these steps:

1. Tap the Search button in the Options bar (refer to Figure 5-2).

A list of possible matches appears (see Figure 5-10).

2. Tap an item in the results.

A page of results on the default search engine is displayed.

3. Tap a result in the search engine results to go to that page.

To specify a search engine to use other than the default, tap the Left Nav button and then tap Settings. Tap the Search Engine option to choose Bing, Google, or Yahoo! as the default search engine.

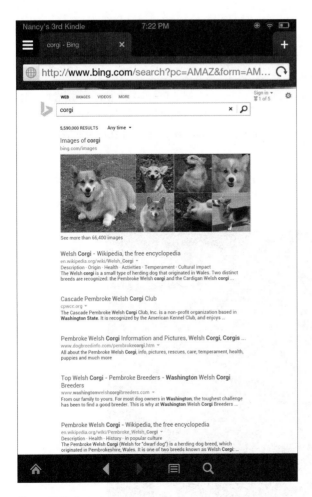

Figure 5-10: Search results are displayed in the default search engine you specify — in this case, Bing.

Reviewing browsing history

We've all experienced this: You know you visited a site in the last day or so that had a great deal, product, news story, or whatever — but you just can't remember the URL of the site. That's where the ability to review your browsing history comes in handy. Using this feature, you can scan the sites you visited recently. They are organized by day, and more often than not, you can spot the place you want to revisit.

With Silk open:

1. Tap the Left Nav button.

2. Tap History.

Sites you've visited on the Kindle Fire HDX appear in a list divided into categories such as Today (see Figure 5-11) and Last 7 Days.

3. Look over these sites, and when you find the one you want, tap it to go there.

To avoid losing a site you know you want to revisit, bookmark it using the procedure outlined in the section "Bookmarking sites," earlier in this chapter.

Nancy's 3rd Kindle	7:36 PM	⊕ 📶 🔋

☰ History   Clear All

˅ Today

7:35PM	Local Weather from AccuWeather.com - Supe...	✕
	http://www.accuweather.com/	
7:33PM	Nanotechnology in Electronics | Nanoelectronics	✕
	http://understandingnano.com/nanotechnology-electr...	
7:28PM	Best tablets - CNET Reviews	✕
	http://reviews.cnet.com/best-tablets/	
7:22PM	corgi - Bing	✕
	http://www.bing.com/search?pc=AMAZ&form=AMAZ...	
7:21PM	CNN.com - Breaking News, U.S., World, Wea...	✕
	http://www.cnn.com/	
7:07PM	Product reviews - Electronics reviews, comput...	✕
	http://reviews.cnet.com/	
7:07PM	Samsung Ativ Book 9 Plus Review - Watch C...	✕
	http://www.cnet.com/laptops/samsung-ativ-book-9/4...	
6:47PM	Laptops & notebooks: Laptop computers, not...	✕
	http://reviews.cnet.com/laptops/	
6:46PM	Laptops - CNET Reviews	✕
	http://reviews.cnet.com/laptop-reviews/	
6:46PM	Best laptops - CNET Reviews	✕
	http://reviews.cnet.com/best-laptops/	
6:45PM	Product reviews and prices, software downloa...	✕
	http://www.cnet.com/	
6:43PM	Nanoparticles | Uses and Applications of Nan...	✕
	http://understandingnano.com/nanoparticles.html	
6:43PM	Nanomaterials	✕
	http://understandingnano.com/nanomaterials.html	
6:43PM	Nanotubes |Carbon Nanotubes	˅

Figure 5-11: To help you find what you want, sites are divided chronologically.

Working with web page content

There are a few things you can do to work with contents of websites using Kindle Fire HDX. For example, you may find online content, such as a PDF file, that you want to download to your Docs library, or an image you want to download to the photo Gallery. You can also open or share content you find online.

Here's how these features work:

- ✐ **View downloads:** Tap the Left Nav button on the Options bar and then tap the Downloads button to view completed downloads.

- ✐ **Save or view images:** Press and hold an image, and a menu appears offering options such as Save Image or View Image (see Figure 5-12).

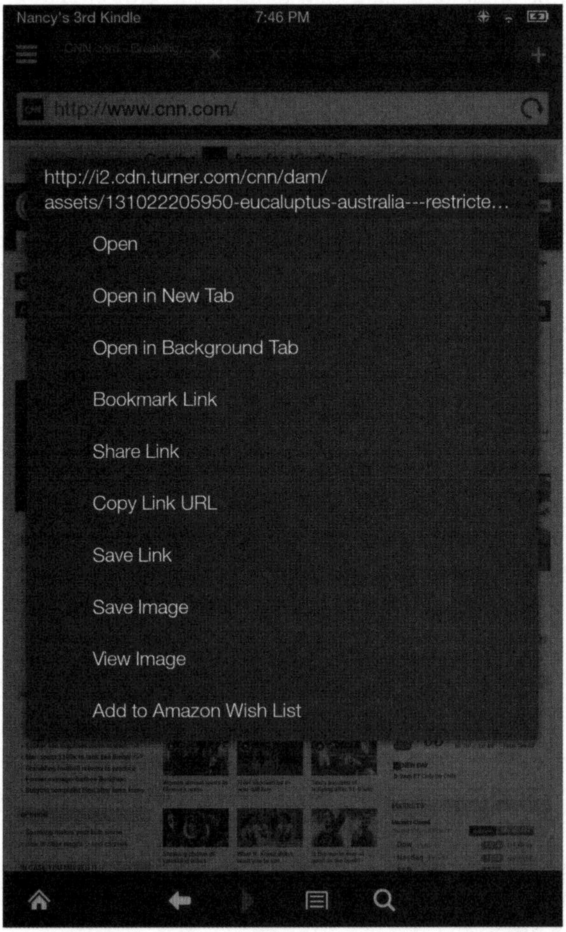

Figure 5-12: You can work with links and images on your Kindle Fire HDX by using this menu.

✔ **Open, save, or share links:** Press and hold your finger on any linked text or image until a menu appears, offering options including Open, Open in New Tab, Open in Background Tab, Bookmark Link, Share Link, Copy Link URL, and Save Link.

Choosing Privacy Settings

Browsing out there on the Internet can be a bit dangerous. There are people and businesses who want to leave small files on your computer called *cookies* that they use to track your activities or gain illegal access to your online accounts.

Some uses of cookies are perfectly legitimate and allow a reputable business such as Amazon to greet you with personalized recommendations based on your past activities when you visit their sites. Less reputable sites sell your information to others or advertise based on your online history by displaying irritating pop-up windows.

The Privacy settings for Silk help you to stay safe when you're browsing online. With Silk open, tap the Left Nav button and then tap Settings to view and modify the following Saved Data settings (see Figure 5-13):

✔ **Clear History:** Your Silk browser retains a history of your browsing activity to make it easy for you to revisit a site. However, it's possible for others who view your browsing history to draw conclusions about your online habits. To clear your history, tap OK in this setting.

✔ **Clear Cache:** Any computing device holds information in its cache, to help it redisplay a page you've visited recently, for example. To clear that cache, which can also free some memory on your Kindle Fire HDX, tap OK.

✔ **Accept Cookies:** Tap this check box to allow sites to download cookies to your Kindle Fire HDX.

✔ **Clear All Cookie Data:** You can tap this setting, and then, in the Clear dialog box that appears, tap OK to clear all cookies from your device.

✔ **Remember Passwords:** This setting saves you the time you'd spend entering usernames and passwords for sites you visit often. Just be aware that this setting puts your accounts at risk should you ever misplace your Kindle Fire HDX. One option, if you use this setting, is to require a password to unlock your Kindle Fire HDX's Home screen. That setting, which can help protect all content stored on the device, is discussed in Chapter 3.

✔ **Clear Passwords:** If you previously allowed Silk to remember passwords but have a change of heart, you can tap OK in this setting to remove saved passwords.

Nancy's 3rd Kindle   7:52 PM

☰ Settings

SAVED DATA

Clear History

Clear Cache

Accept Cookies ✓

Clear All Cookie Data

Remember Passwords ✓
Save user names and passwords for websites.

Clear Passwords
Forget all saved website passwords on this device.

Remember Form Data ✓
Remember data typed in forms for later use.

Clear Form Data

Enable Location ✓
Allow sites to request access to your location.

Clear Location Access

Individual Website Data
Advanced settings for individual websites.

Figure 5-13: Privacy settings can protect your personal information as you browse.

> ✔ **Remember Form Data:** If you want Silk to remember data you've entered into forms before — such as your name, mailing address, or e-mail address — to help you complete online fields more quickly, tap this check box. The danger here, and the reason you might choose to deselect this check box, is that if somebody gets ahold of your Kindle Fire HDX, that person could use this feature to gain access to some of your personal information or use your online accounts.
>
> ✔ **Clear Form Data:** Clears out any form data you've already saved.
>
> ✔ **Enable Location:** Tap this check box to allow websites to request information about your physical location.
>
> ✔ **Clear Location Access:** If you don't want websites to know your physical location (often used to push ads at you that relate to your location), tap this and then tap OK to clear access.

✔ **Individual Website Data:** Tap this to gain access to a setting to clear data for an individual website you've visited.

✔ **Prompt Before Download:** Turn this feature on to be asked to confirm downloads. This is useful because some sites initiate downloads even if you don't request them, and those downloads could contain malware.

If you want to get rid of all the settings you've selected in Silk, with Silk open, tap the Left Nav button and then tap Settings. Scroll down to Advanced Settings and then tap Reset All Settings to Default.

Working with E-Mail

Kindle Fire HDX has a built-in e-mail client. A *client* essentially allows you to access e-mail accounts you've set up through various providers, such as Gmail and Yahoo!. You can then open the inboxes of these accounts and read, reply to, and forward messages by using your Kindle Fire HDX. You can also create and send new messages, and even include attachments.

The latest Kindle e-mail app supports accounts with Outlook, Yahoo!, AOL, and more. You can also group e-mail conversations by subject.

In the following sections, I provide information about setting up and using your e-mail accounts on Kindle Fire HDX.

Setting up an e-mail account

Setting up your e-mail on Kindle Fire HDX involves providing information about one or more e-mail accounts that you've already established with a provider such as Gmail.

Follow these steps to set up an e-mail account the first time you use the app:

1. **Tap Email in the Favorites Grid.**

   The Mail app appears.

2. **From the Inbox, tap the Left Nav button.**

   The Settings panel appears.

3. **Tap Settings.**

4. **Tap Add Account.**

   The dialog box shown in Figure 5-14 appears.

5. **Enter your e-mail address and then tap Next.**

6. **Enter your password and then tap Next.**

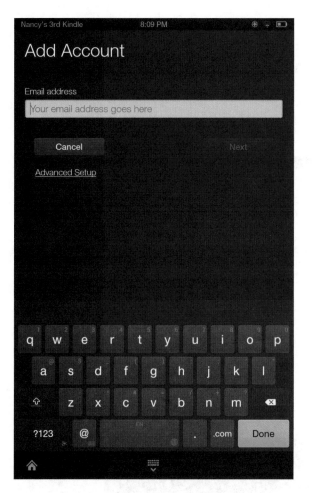

Figure 5-14: Choose your e-mail account.

7. **Kindle Fire HDX verifies your account and displays a Setup Complete screen, where you can choose to go to the e-mail Inbox or add another account.**

You can set up as many e-mail accounts as you like. When you open the Kindle Fire HDX Email app, you see a Unified Inbox that combines messages from all accounts you set up, as well as individual Inboxes for each account.

Sending e-mail

After you set up your e-mail account(s), as described in the preceding section, you're able to send e-mails from your Kindle Fire HDX. To create and send an e-mail, with the Email app and an e-mail account Inbox open, follow these steps:

1. **Tap the New button.**

   A blank e-mail form appears, as shown in Figure 5-15.

2. **In the To field, enter a name.**

   Alternatively, tap the Add Contact button (+) to open the Contacts app and tap a name there to add that person as an addressee (assuming that the Contact record includes an e-mail address).

Figure 5-15: A blank form waiting for you to enter an e-mail address, subject, and message.

3. **If you want to send a copy of the e-mail to somebody, tap the Cc/Bcc button to make those fields appear; then enter addresses or choose them from the Contacts app by tapping the Add Contact button.**

4. **Tap in the Subject field and enter a subject by using the onscreen keyboard.**

5. **Tap in the Message text field and enter a message.**

6. **(Optional) If you want to add an attachment to an e-mail, tap the Menu button to the right of the Send button and, in the menu that appears, choose Attach Photo or Attach File and choose a file from the sources offered.**

7. **To send your message, tap the Send button.**

   If you decide you're not ready to send the message quite yet, you also have the option of tapping the Menu button and then tapping Save Draft.

Here are a couple of handy shortcuts for entering text in your e-mail: The Auto Complete feature lists possible word matches along the top of the onscreen keyboard as you type; tap one to complete a word. In addition, you can double-tap the spacebar to place a period and space at the end of a sentence.

Receiving e-mail

Kindle Fire HDX can receive your e-mail messages whenever you're connected to a Wi-Fi network.

When an e-mail is delivered to your Inbox (see Figure 5-16), simply tap to open it. Read it and contemplate whether you want to save it or delete it (or forward or reply to it, as covered in the following section). If you don't need to keep the message, you can delete it by tapping the Delete button at the top of the screen.

Forwarding and replying to e-mail

When you receive an e-mail, you can choose to reply to the sender, reply to the sender and anybody else who was included as an addressee on the original message, or forward the e-mail to another person.

If you reply to all recipients, you send an answer to the sender, anybody else in the To field of the original message, and anybody in the Cc and Bcc fields. Because Bcc fields aren't visible to you as a recipient, you may be sending your reply to people you're not aware of.

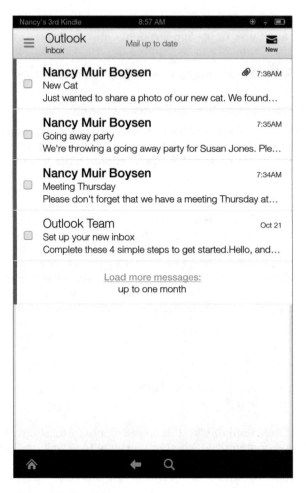

Figure 5-16: Your Inbox.

To forward or reply to an e-mail, with the Email app Inbox displayed, follow these steps:

1. **Tap an e-mail to open it.**

2. **Tap Reply, Reply All, or Forward (see Figure 5-17).**

3. **If you're forwarding the message, enter a new recipient.**

   If you're replying, the message is already addressed, but you can enter additional recipients if you want.

4. **Tap in the message area and enter your message.**

5. **Tap the Send button to send your message on its way.**

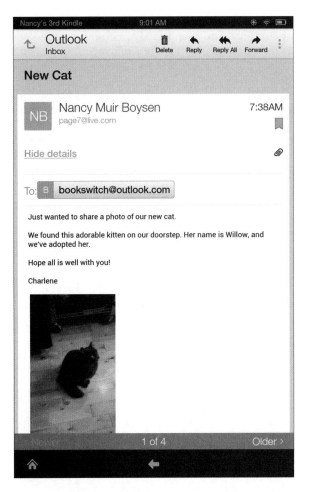

Figure 5-17: Choose to reply to a message or send it on to somebody else.

When you read a message, you can tell that it has been marked as read when the sender's name is no longer shown in bold. To mark it as unread again, perhaps to draw your attention to it so you read it again, tap the Menu button in the top right corner of the screen and then tap the Mark Unread button in the menu that appears.

Sending E-Mail to Your Kindle Account

When you register your Kindle Fire HDX, you get an associated e-mail account, which essentially allows you or others to e-mail documents in Word, PDF, RTF, or HTML format to your Kindle Fire HDX.

The address of the account is displayed when you swipe down to display Quick Settings, tap Settings, and then tap My Account; you see your name, and underneath is the name of your Kindle e-mail account (*yourname*@kindle. com).

You or others can e-mail documents to this address, and those documents automatically appear in your Docs library. Note that you might need to go to Amazon.com by using a browser and change the approved e-mail accounts. From your computer, click Your Account and then Manage Your Kindle in the menu that appears. Click the Personal Document Settings link on the left side of the screen and make sure that the account is listed under Send to Kindle Email Settings.

Part III

Having Fun and Getting Productive

Visit www.dummies.com/extras/kindlefirehdx to read an article with tips on how to get more out of the built-in OfficeSuite.

In this part...

- ✐ Use your Kindle Fire HDX as an e-reader.
- ✐ Buy and play music.
- ✐ Have fun watching movies and TV shows.
- ✐ Enjoy interaction with social networking services Facebook and Twitter.
- ✐ Use useful apps such as Calendar and OfficeSuite Pro to be more productive.

6

E-Reader Extraordinaire

In This Chapter

▶ Looking into what's available to read

▶ Borrowing and lending books

▶ Opening a good book

▶ Flipping through periodicals

▶ Looking at docs on Kindle Fire HDX

Kindle Fire HDX comes from a family of e-readers, so it's only natural that the e-reader you use to read books and magazines on the device is a very robust feature. With its bright, colorful screen, Kindle Fire HDX broadens your reading experience beyond black-and-white books to color publications such as magazines or graphic novels. Its easy-to-use controls help you navigate publications, bookmark and highlight text, and search your libraries of print content.

X-Ray now works with selected books. When a book is X-Ray – enabled, you can view information about characters in the book and jump to places in the book where they appear. You can also get information about locations and important terms.

In this chapter, you can discover what's available, how to open publications, and how to read and then delete them from Kindle Fire HDX when you're done. You also explore the possibilities of Amazon's lending library and how to lend books to your friends and borrow books from your local public library.

So Many Things to Read!

Amazon started as an online book retailer, although through the years it has branched out to become the largest retailer of just about everything on the planet. Kindle Fire HDX makes it easy for you to buy your content from Amazon. Although you can buy and sideload content from other sources to Kindle Fire HDX, buying from Amazon ensures that you're dealing with a reputable company and receiving safe content (uncontaminated by malware).

The content you buy from Amazon is automatically downloaded to your Kindle device, which means that not only is buying from the Amazon Bookstore easy but also that you can take advantage of its vast selection of books. In addition, you can borrow Kindle versions of books from the Amazon Lending Library as well as many public libraries. You can also lend books to your friends.

Amazon has also made deals to make many of your favorite magazines and newspapers available. With magazines and newspapers, you can buy the current issue or subscribe to get multiple issues sent to your Kindle Fire HDX as they become available.

Goodreads is an app you can download for free that offers a sort of virtual book club. You can share content, reviews, and recommendations with others, and access other peoples' reviews and recommendations. Download the Goodreads app to get started.

Buying books

To buy books or magazines for your Kindle Fire HDX, on the Home screen, tap either the Books or Newsstand button, which takes you to your Books or Magazine library.

Tap the Store button; this takes you to the Amazon Kindle Bookstore, shown in Figure 6-1. See Chapter 4 for more about how to search for and buy content.

You can also buy content at the Amazon website from your computer and have it download to your Kindle Fire HDX. Just select what device you want it delivered to from the drop-down list below the Add to Cart button before you buy Kindle content.

Amazon uses a technology called Whispersync to download books and magazines to your devices. All Wi-Fi – only models of Kindle Fire HDX require a Wi-Fi connection, so you need to be connected to a Wi-Fi hotspot to download publications. Whispersync for Voice is a technology that syncs between a printed book and audiobook if you own both. You can leave off reading in the print book, for example, and when you next start your audiobook, it will pick up where you left off.

A new feature called Matchbook was in the wings at the time of writing this book. Using Matchbook, you can buy a print edition of a qualifying book and then buy the Kindle version for $0.99 to $2.99. Some will even be free.

Figure 6-1: Buy books at the Amazon Kindle Bookstore.

Using the Amazon Lending Library

On the screen that appears when you enter the store (see the preceding section), follow these steps to borrow a book:

1. **Tap the Left Nav button.**

2. **Tap the Kindle Lending Library link.**

A list of free lending selections appears (see Figure 6-2).

These free items are available only if you have an Amazon Prime membership. You get 30 days of Prime free when you buy your Kindle Fire HDX.

3. **Tap an item to make a descriptive page appear.**

4. **Tap the Borrow for Free button.**

Your selection is immediately downloaded.

You can borrow a title from the Lending Library every 14 days.

If you want to borrow Kindle books on other devices such as your PC, you can do so if you download the Kindle reading app.

Figure 6-2: These and many more selections are free if you have an Amazon Prime account.

For selected titles that you've bought in Kindle format, you can lend them to others for a period of 14 days. Go to the product detail page on Amazon.com and click Loan This Book. On the Loan This Book page, enter an e-mail address for the person you're lending the book to. Enter a personal message if you like, and then click Send Now. Remember, this feature is available only for some books, not all, and a book can be loaned only once.

Borrowing from your local library

More than 11,000 libraries in the United States lend Kindle versions of books through a system called Overdrive, which allows you to easily download books to your Kindle Fire HDX. The length of time for which you can borrow a book varies by library, and each library may have a slightly different system for borrowing books. You typically initiate the library loan from the library's website, enter your Amazon account information, and then specify the device to deliver the book to.

Here are the typical steps for borrowing Kindle books from your library, but you should ask your library for the specific steps that work with its system:

1. Go to your library's website and search for e-books.

   Note that you'll need a library card and PIN to borrow books.

2. Click the title you want to check out and then enter your library card information and PIN.

3. After you check out a title, choose the Get for Kindle option.
   You may then have to enter your Amazon.com account information to borrow the title.

4. Choose the title and your Kindle Fire HDX as the device you want the book delivered to; then choose Get Library Book to download the title.

Reading Books

After you own some Kindle books, you can begin to read by using the simple e-reader tools in the Kindle e-reader app. You may have used this app on another device, such as your computer, smartphone, or other tablet, though each version of this app has slightly different features. In the following sections, I go over the basics of how the Kindle e-reader app works on Kindle Fire HDX.

You can get to the Home screen from anywhere in the e-reader app. If a Home button isn't visible, just tap the page to display the Options bar, which includes a Home button and a set of tools for navigating a book.

Going to the (Books) library

When you tap Books on your Kindle Fire HDX screen, you open the Books library, containing downloaded content on the On Device tab and content in the Cloud on the Cloud tab (see Figure 6-3). The active tab is the one displaying an orange underline. There's also a Store button that you use to go to Amazon's website to shop for books.

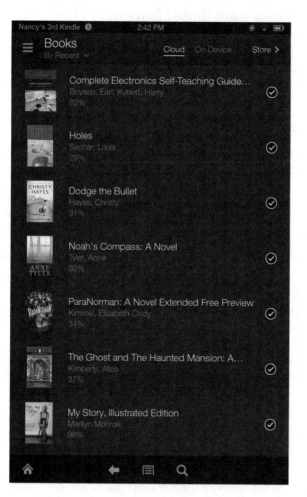

Figure 6-3: The Books library displays all your book purchases and library loans on two tabs.

There are also several features in your Books library that you can use to get different perspectives on its contents:

✔ **Grid and List views:** Tap the Menu button on the Options bar to display an option that allows you to toggle between the Grid View

and List View options. These provide views of your books by using
large thumbnails on a bookshelf (Grid view, shown in Figure 6-4)
or in a text list including title and author, along with an accompanying
small thumbnail.

Figure 6-4: The Grid view in the Books library.

- ✔ **Sort titles:** Use the drop-down list under the Books library title to select
  By Author, By Recent, and By Title to view books by any of these three
  criteria.

- ✔ **Identify new titles:** If you've just downloaded but haven't started reading
  a book, there will be a banner in the corner of the thumbnail with the word
  New on it (see Figure 6-5).

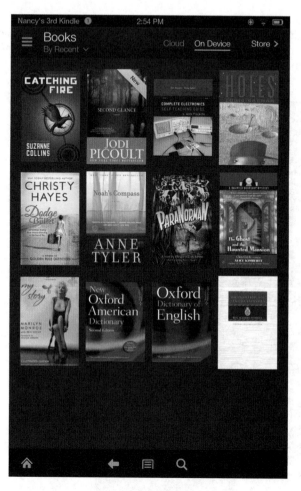

Figure 6-5: New titles are easily identifiable.

Tap the Search button on the Options bar to search your Books library contents by title or author.

Opening a book

Ah, the pleasure you had as a child in opening up a new book, awaiting the adventures or knowledge it had to impart! Opening your first e-book is likely to bring you a similar sort of pleasure.

To open a book from the Home screen, follow these steps:

1. **Tap Books.**

   The Books library opens.

2. **Locate the book you want to read (swipe upward if you need to reveal more books in the list).**

3. **Tap a book.**

   If the book has not been downloaded to your Kindle Fire HDX, it begins to download and takes only seconds to complete.

If you never started to read the book, it opens on its title page. If you've read part of the book, it opens automatically to the last page you read. This last-read page is bookmarked in the Cloud by Amazon when you stop reading, so no matter what device you use to read it — your Kindle Fire HDX, computer, or smartphone, for example — you go to the last-read page immediately.

You can also open a publication from Favorites or the Carousel. Read more about these features in Chapter 2.

Navigating a book

An open book just begs to be read. You're used to flipping pages in a physical book, but an e-reader provides you with several ways to move around.

The simplest way to move one page forward or one page back is to tap or swipe your finger anywhere on the right or left side of the page, respectively. Try this to move from the title page to a page of text within the book.

With a book page displayed, tap it to see these buttons in the Options bar along the top of the screen (see Figure 6-6):

- ✔ **Home:** Located in the bottom-left corner, this button takes you to the Kindle Fire HDX Home screen.

- ✔ **Back:** Tap the button of a left-pointing arrow to go back one screen (not page).

- ✔ **Search:** Use the magnifying glass button found in the middle of the screen to initiate a search for text in the book.

In addition to the items in the Options bar at the bottom of the screen, you find these tools along the top of the screen:

- ✔ **View:** Use this button to access settings for font, background, and text spacing.

- ✔ **Text:** This button displays a menu of options for formatting text, choosing the page background, and more.

- ✔ **X-Ray:** Tap this button to view additional information about the book if it's available for that title.

- ✔ **Notes:** Displays any notes you have made in the book.

✔ **Share:** Use this button to share your thoughts about the book via Twitter or Facebook.

✔ **Bookmark:** Places a bookmark on the page.

You can also tap the Left Nav button, the leftmost button, which contains options you can tap to

✔ Go to a particular page or location in the book.

✔ Sync to the last page you read on any device.

✔ Jump to the book title page, table of contents, or individual chapter titles.

✔ View more information about the author. This includes two options, A Note About the Author and Other Books By This Author.

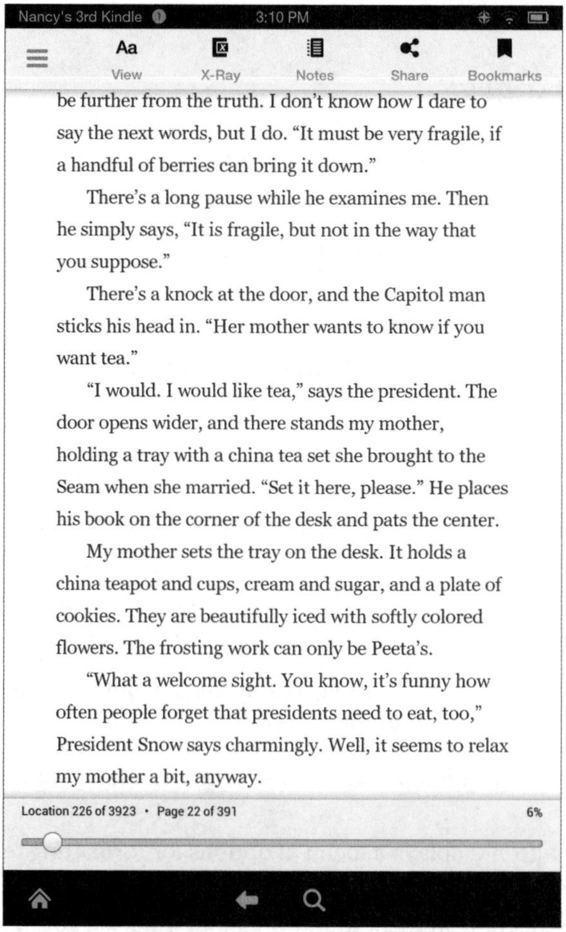

Figure 6-6: A typical page of a book in Kindle e-reader.

Reading children's books

Many children's books with extensive illustrations use what Amazon refers to as a *fixed layout,* meaning that the pages are fixed representations of how the pages look in the print book. This means that you can't enlarge and reduce the size of everything on the page at one time, you can't change the font style, and you can't change orientation: Each book is set in either landscape or portrait orientation. To move from page to page, you can swipe from right to left on the right page to flip it over.

Keep in mind that children's books are usually set up with blocks of text that go along with illustrations; that's why you can't enlarge all the text on an entire page. Instead, you enlarge a single block of text. To do this, double-tap a block of text, and the text becomes larger. When you subsequently swipe the page, you move to the next block of text, which enlarges (the previous block of text goes back to normal size). When you've read the last block of text on the page (typically in a two-page spread), swiping takes you to the next page. Double-tap the currently enlarged text again to go back to normal text size and proceed through the book.

The Progress bar along the bottom of the screen (refer to Figure 6-6) indicates how far along in the publication you are at the moment. To move around the publication, you can press the circle on this bar and drag it in either direction.

Diving In with Immersion Reading

Immersion Reading lets you buy the narration from an audiobook to go along with a print book you own. When you do, you can play the professional narration from your book, and text is highlighted as each word is spoken. This so-called Immersion Reading approach is supposed to help reader retention and plunge you deep into the reading experience.

To use Immersion Reading:

1. **Go to** www.amazon.com. You can use your computer for this or your Silk browser from Kindle Fire. These steps are based on using a computer without touchscreen.

2. **Click Shop by Department⇨Audible Audiobooks⇨Whispersync for Voice.**

   A selection of books that are Immersion Reading–enabled appears.

3. **Locate the book you want to buy and click Buy or Buy with 1-Click, depending on how your account is set up.**

   If you choose Buy, you are presented with a price button; click it.

4. **You're asked if you want to buy the narration; click to buy the narration.**

5. **From the Kindle Fire HDX Home screen, tap Books.**

6. **In your library, tap to open the Immersion Reading–enabled book.**

7. **In the screen that appears (see Figure 6-7), tap the Play button at the bottom of the screen to play the narration.**

   Each word is highlighted as it's spoken.

8. **Tap the Pause button when you're ready to pause the audio playback.**

You can also download the free Audible app, and after signing in with your Amazon account information, download audiobooks from the My Library area of the app.

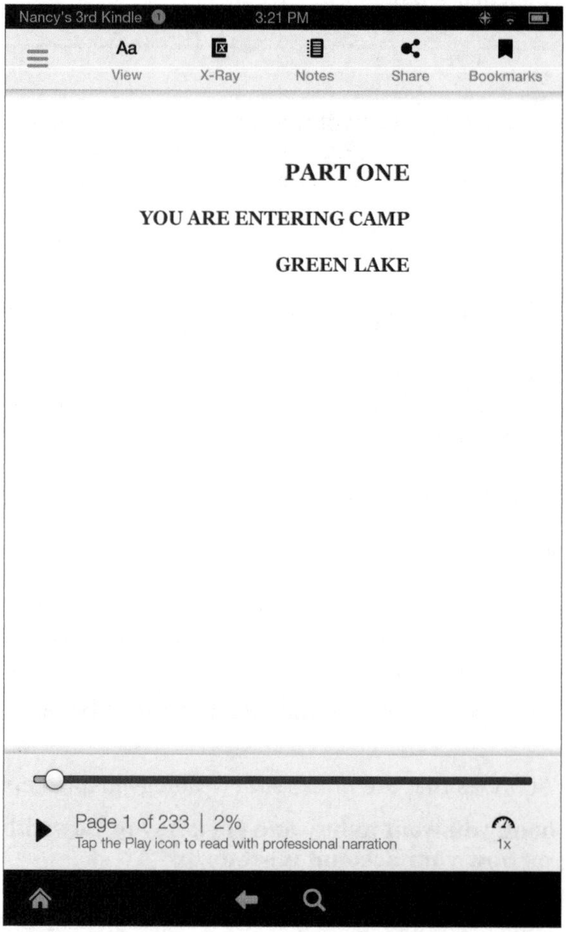

Nancy's 3rd Kindle ❶   3:21 PM

≡	Aa	⬚	▤	⚞	▮
	View	X-Ray	Notes	Share	Bookmarks

PART ONE

YOU ARE ENTERING CAMP

GREEN LAKE

▶ Page 1 of 233 | 2%
Tap the Play icon to read with professional narration   1x

Figure 6-7: Play the narration of the audiobook from right within your Books library.

X-Ray for Books

Although only some books are X-Ray enabled at this point in time, if you find one that is, you can get information about characters and their back stories, as well as locations and other terms mentioned in the book.

Here's how to use X-Ray with books:

1. **Open a book that is X-Ray enabled, like the one shown in Figure 6-8.**

2. **Tap the top of the screen to display the toolbar shown in the figure.**

   You see an X-Ray button.

3. **Tap the X-Ray button.**

   You see a list of items in the book.

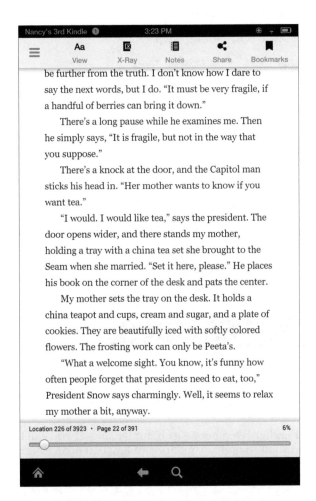

Figure 6-8: A book with the X-Ray button available.

4. Tap All to see all people and terms; People to see just information about characters in the book; and Terms to see only locations and key terms (see Figure 6-9).

5. Tap the blue spots on the bar to the right of each item to go to different locations in the book where that item is mentioned.

Figure 6-9: Get information about characters and locations.

Searching in a book

Want to find that earlier reference to a character so that you can keep up with a plot? Or do you want to find any mention of Einstein in an e-encyclopedia? To find words or phrases in a book, you can use the Search feature.

Follow these steps to search a book:

1. **With a book open, tap the page to display the Options bar, if necessary.**
2. **Tap the Search button at the bottom of the page.**

   If you're holding Kindle Fire in landscape orientation, the Search button is on the right side. The Search field and onscreen keyboard are displayed, as shown in Figure 6-10.

3. **Enter a search term or phrase and then tap the Go key on the keyboard.**

   Search results are displayed, as shown in Figure 6-11.

Figure 6-10: Search for a word or phrase by using the Search field and onscreen keyboard.

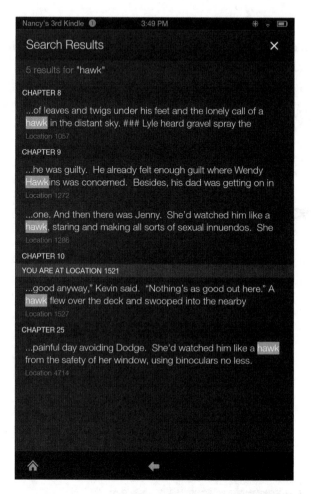

Figure 6-11: Search results indicate the search term with a highlight.

If you'd rather search the web, press a word or phrase to highlight it, and then in the resulting dialog box, tap the More button. At this point, you can tap either Search in Book, Search Wikipedia, or Search the Web. The Search the Web option takes you to search results for the term in the Bing search engine, and the Wikipedia option takes you to the entry in the popular online encyclopedia that matches your search term. Tap the Back button when you want to return to the e-reader app.

You may have noticed that the progress bar in a book shows a pretty incomprehensible location number, not a page number. This number is related to where you are in the set of data contained in a book and is pretty meaningless to a reader. An Amazon representative has told me that they're looking into changing this number to a page number; let's hope it's soon!

Bookmarking a page and highlighting text

If you find that perfect quote or a phrase that you just have to read again at a later time, you can use the Bookmark feature in Kindle e-reader.

To place a bookmark on a page, display the page and tap near the top edge of the right corner of a page. A small bookmark ribbon appears on the page (see Figure 6-12). Tap the ribbon to remove it.

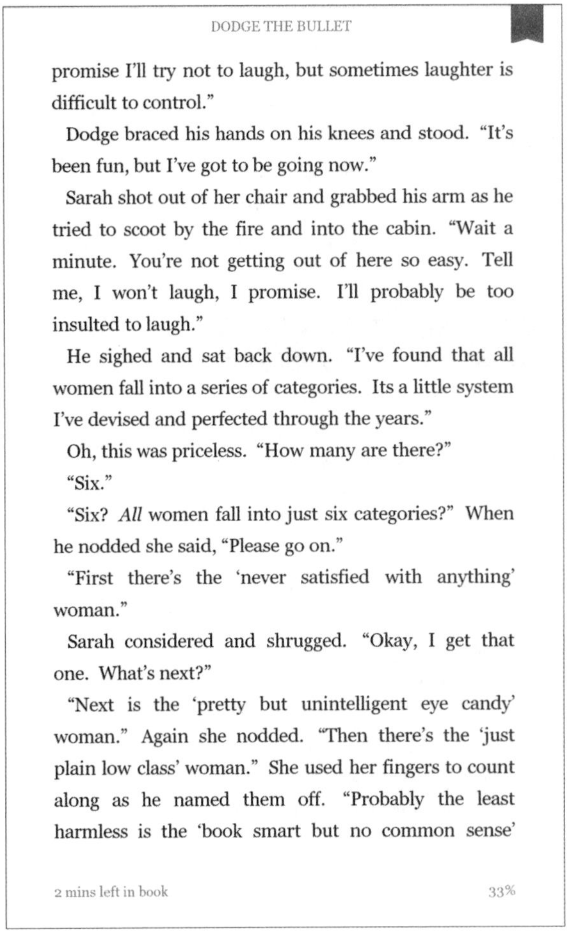

DODGE THE BULLET

promise I'll try not to laugh, but sometimes laughter is difficult to control."

Dodge braced his hands on his knees and stood. "It's been fun, but I've got to be going now."

Sarah shot out of her chair and grabbed his arm as he tried to scoot by the fire and into the cabin. "Wait a minute. You're not getting out of here so easy. Tell me, I won't laugh, I promise. I'll probably be too insulted to laugh."

He sighed and sat back down. "I've found that all women fall into a series of categories. Its a little system I've devised and perfected through the years."

Oh, this was priceless. "How many are there?"

"Six."

"Six? *All* women fall into just six categories?" When he nodded she said, "Please go on."

"First there's the 'never satisfied with anything' woman."

Sarah considered and shrugged. "Okay, I get that one. What's next?"

"Next is the 'pretty but unintelligent eye candy' woman." Again she nodded. "Then there's the 'just plain low class' woman." She used her fingers to count along as he named them off. "Probably the least harmless is the 'book smart but no common sense'

2 mins left in book   33%

Figure 6-12: A bookmarked page.

To highlight text:

1. **Press and hold your finger on the text.**

   Small handles appear on either side.

2. **If you want to select additional adjacent text to be highlighted, press your finger on one of these triangular handles and drag to the left or right.**

3. **When the entire phrase or paragraph you want to highlight is selected, remove your finger.**

   A dialog box appears (see Figure 6-13).

4. **Tap one of the colored highlight boxes.**

   The text is highlighted using the selected color.

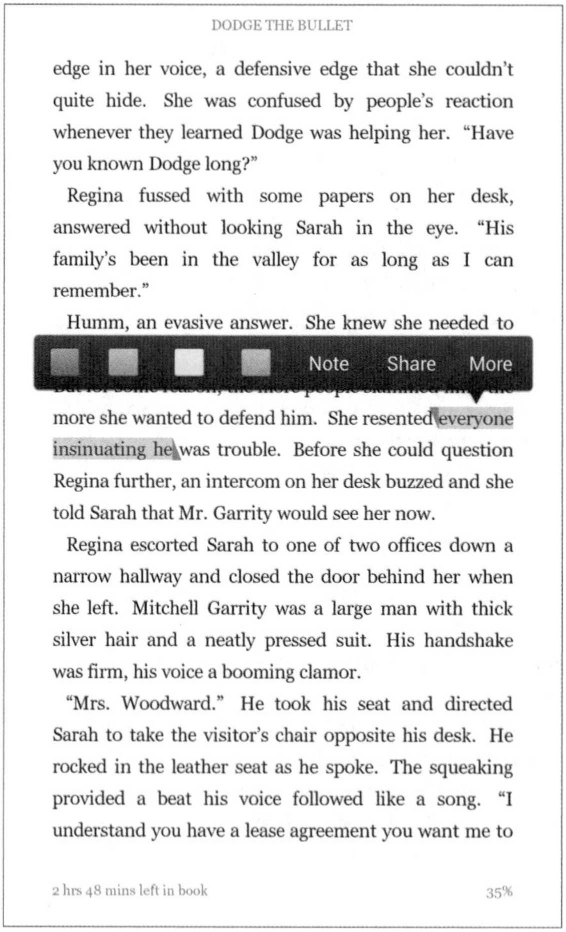

DODGE THE BULLET

edge in her voice, a defensive edge that she couldn't quite hide. She was confused by people's reaction whenever they learned Dodge was helping her. "Have you known Dodge long?"

Regina fussed with some papers on her desk, answered without looking Sarah in the eye. "His family's been in the valley for as long as I can remember."

Humm, an evasive answer. She knew she needed to

Note   Share   More

more she wanted to defend him. She resented everyone insinuating he was trouble. Before she could question Regina further, an intercom on her desk buzzed and she told Sarah that Mr. Garrity would see her now.

Regina escorted Sarah to one of two offices down a narrow hallway and closed the door behind her when she left. Mitchell Garrity was a large man with thick silver hair and a neatly pressed suit. His handshake was firm, his voice a booming clamor.

"Mrs. Woodward." He took his seat and directed Sarah to take the visitor's chair opposite his desk. He rocked in the leather seat as he spoke. The squeaking provided a beat his voice followed like a song. "I understand you have a lease agreement you want me to

2 hrs 48 mins left in book   35%

Figure 6-13: Tap either handle to enlarge the area of selected text.

When you place a bookmark on a page or highlight text within a book, you can then display a list of bookmarks and highlights by tapping the page and then tapping the Notes button at the top of the page to display your notes and marks (see Figure 6-14). You can jump to the page indicated by a bookmark or to highlighted text by tapping an item in this list.

Nancy's 3rd Kindle ⓘ   4:17 PM   ⊕ 🛜 ▭

My Notes & Marks   ✕

"I'm sorry to hear that. You know I think that property of yours is a diamond in the rough. I'm
🔖 Bookmark   Location 832

impossibly
◼ Highlight   Location 923

Water would make every acre of land fertile.
◼ Highlight   Location 1001

twitched in annoyance. "As witnessed by your sister. I've got cattle all over the valley, small tracts here and there
🔖 Bookmark   Location 1544

everyone insinuating he was trouble.
◼ Highlight   Location 1716

attention
◼ Highlight   Location 1831

⌂   ⬅

Figure 6-14: Both highlights and bookmarks are listed.

When you press text and see the menu shown in Figure 6-13, a brief definition appears from the pre-installed New Oxford American Dictionary. In the definition window, tap Full Definition to go to the full Oxford dictionary definition. Tap the Back button to return to the book. See Chapter 10 for more about Kindle Fire HDX's built-in dictionary.

Modifying the appearance of a page

There are several things you can do to control how things appear on a page in Kindle e-reader. First, you can make text larger or smaller and change the font. Second, you can choose a white, black, or sepia-toned background for a page. Finally, you can adjust the width of margins and spacing between lines

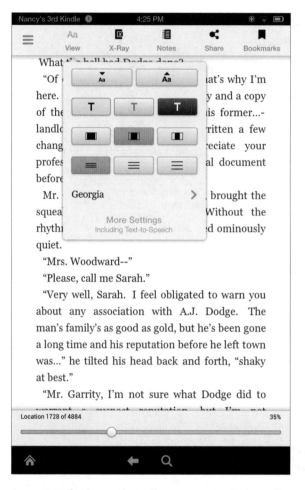

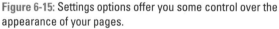

Figure 6-15: Settings options offer you some control over the appearance of your pages.

To control all these settings, tap the page to display the tools, and then tap the View button (the one with Aa, a capital and lowercase A) in the top-left corner of the screen. The options shown in Figure 6-15 appear:

- **Font Size:** Tap a particular font sample to change the size. Tap the down arrow to decrease the size and the up arrow to increase it.

- **Color Mode:** Tap a setting to display a different color for the page background. A white background gives you black text on a white page. A black background gives you white text on a black page. A sepia background gives you a pale tan background and black text, which may make reading easier on your eyes.

✓ **Margins:** Choose the margin setting you prefer.

✓ **Line Spacing:** Tap to select more or less space between lines.

✓ **Font:** Select a different font for the page.

If you tap More Settings in the dialog box shown in Figure 6-15, the Text-to-Speech setting is available. This setting allows you turn on a feature that reads text to you in English for titles that have this feature enabled. With an enabled e-book displayed, tap to display the Progress bar and tools along the top, and then tap the Play button to the left of the Progress bar. The audio begins. Tap the screen and then tap the Pause button to stop the Text-to-Speech feature.

You can adjust brightness manually or have Kindle Fire HDX do it automatically. Go to the Home screen and swipe down from the top of the screen to reveal the Quick Settings bar; then tap the Brightness button. If you turn Automatic Brightness on, the Kindle Fire HDX adjusts the brightness of the screen to compensate for ambient light conditions. If you turn Automatic Brightness off, you can press the circle on the slider and move it to the left or right to adjust brightness.

Sharing with others through Facebook or Twitter

When you're reading a book, you can share your thoughts with others via Facebook or Twitter and let them know how you liked the book. Follow these steps to share your thoughts on a book:

1. **With a book open, tap the screen to display the tools shown in Figure 6-16.**

2. **Tap the Share button near the top-right corner of the screen.**

3. **In the screen that appears (see Figure 6-17), tap to select an account to connect with (Twitter or Facebook).**

   If asked, enter your e-mail account and password to connect to the service.

4. **Tap in the text field at the top of the page and then use the onscreen keyboard to enter a message.**

5. **Tap the Share button to share your thoughts on the book with others.**

Managing Publications

After you purchase content on Amazon, from apps to music and books, that content is archived in your Amazon Cloud library. If you finish reading a book on Kindle Fire HDX, you can remove it from your device. The book is still in the Amazon Cloud, and you can redownload it to your Kindle Fire HDX at any time when you're connected to a Wi-Fi network.

To remove a book or magazine from your Kindle Fire HDX libraries, follow these steps:

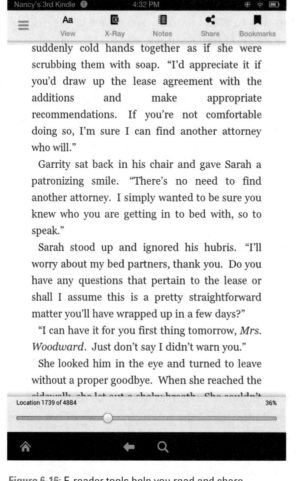

Figure 6-16: E-reader tools help you read and share your thoughts.

1. **On the Home screen, tap Books or Newsstand to display your library.**
2. **Locate and press your finger on the item you want to remove.**

   A menu appears (see Figure 6-18).
3. **Tap Remove from Device.**

The thumbnail of the item remains in your Books library on the Cloud tab and on the Carousel or Favorites if you've placed it there, but it's gone from the On Device tab. To download and read the book again, just double-tap it in any of these locations, and the download begins.

Figure 6-17: Share your thoughts with the Kindle community.

Unlike video and music, which you can stream from the Cloud without ever downloading them, books, magazines, and newspapers can't be read from the Cloud; they must be downloaded to a Kindle device before you can read them.

If you download a periodical and then press your finger on it in Newsstand, you see the Keep or Remove from Device options shown in Figure 6-18. At some point, old issues will be removed from your device unless you choose to keep them by using the Keep command.

Book samples will offer only a Delete option when you get to Step 3 above. The New Oxford American Dictionary offers only the option of Add to Home to add it to the Favorites grid because it's pre-installed by Amazon.

Figure 6-18: Use this menu to remove a publication from Kindle Fire HDX.

Buying and Reading Periodicals

Reading magazines and newspapers on your Kindle Fire HDX is similar to reading books, with a few important differences. You navigate magazines a bit differently and can display them in two different views.

Follow these steps to buy and read a magazine or newspaper:

1. **From the Home screen, tap Newsstand.**

2. **Tap Store.**

3. **Tap a periodical and then tap Subscribe Now or Buy Issue to buy it.**

4. **Return to Newsstand and tap a magazine or newspaper in the Newsstand to read it.**

   Alternatively, you can tap an item on the Carousel from the Home screen.

   If the publication hasn't been downloaded to the device, it begins to download now.

5. **Tap the screen to display the Options bar and tools and then tap the Browse button to display thumbnails of pages (see Figure 6-19).**

Figure 6-19: Scroll through thumbnails of pages to find the one you want.

6. **Tap the screen to display a page, and then swipe right or left to scroll through these pages or drag the scroll bar indicator left or right.**

7. **Tap the Left Nav button to display the articles in the publications.**

8. **Tap an item in the list to go to that item.**

As with books, in most publications you can double-tap to enlarge text on the page; double-tap again to reduce the size of the text. You can also pinch and unpinch the touchscreen to move between larger and smaller views of a page's contents.

Reading Docs on Kindle Fire HDX

Reading documents on your Kindle Fire HDX is a much more straightforward proposition than reading e-books (meaning that there are fewer things you can do to navigate around a document or format the appearance of text). You can get docs onto your Kindle Fire HDX by e-mailing them as attachments to your Kindle e-mail account, or by transferring them from another device after you've connected it with the Kindle Fire HDX using the USB cord. On your computer, for example, you can just find the document you want and drag it to your Docs folder.

Tap the Docs button on the Home screen and then locate and tap a document; or tap a doc on the Carousel or Favorites to open it.

Swipe left or right to move from page to page or use the thumbnails that appear along the bottom of the screen when the Options bar is displayed to move around the document.

In OfficeSuite docs, you can make notes and highlights, but you can't do this in PDF documents. To make notes and highlights in an OfficeSuite doc, press a word to display a menu and then tap Note or tap a Highlight color in that menu. You can read more about docs and Kindle Fire HDX in Chapter 10.

Playing Music

In This Chapter

▶ Checking out the Music library

▶ Getting music onto the Cloud

▶ Listening to music using your Kindle Fire HDX

Music has become ubiquitous in most of our lives. Portable devices provide us with decent-quality sound systems for listening to everything from Lady Gaga to Mozart, everywhere from the subway to the jogging path.

The ability to tap into Amazon's tremendous Music store (with more than 20 million songs at the time of this writing) and access it from any device including your Kindle Fire HDX means that you can build up your ideal music library and take it with you wherever you go. You can also *sideload* (transfer) music from other sources into your Kindle Fire by using the provided micro USB cable.

Also, the addition of Dolby Digital Plus, audio powered through dual-driver stereo speakers that come with Kindle Fire HD and HDX, provides one of the finest listening experiences in the world of tablets. This system even optimizes sound for what you're playing so that music sounds like music rather than movie dialog. Music played through Kindle Fire HDX's speakers sounds great, and music through headsets is optimized for that listening environment.

In this chapter, you learn about getting music onto your Kindle Fire HDX (see Chapter 4 for more about shopping for music) and how to use the simple tools in the library to play your music and create playlists.

Exploring the Music Library

All your music is stored in the Music library (see Figure 7-1), which you display by tapping the Music button on the Kindle Fire HDX Home screen. The currently playing or last played song is displayed along with playback controls located at the bottom of the screen.

The library can be organized by Playlists, Artists (as shown in Figure 7-2), Albums, Songs, or Genres. Tap the Left Nav button and then tap any of these categories to display the associated content.

Explore the Cloud Collection feature to organize all your content into collections via Amazon Cloud. See Chapter 4 for more about this feature, which comes new with Fire OS 3.0.

Figure 7-1: The Music library is your central music repository.

Figure 7-2: The Artists category shows available content by performer.

At the bottom of the screen, in the Options bar, is a back arrow; when you're playing a musical selection, tapping this moves you back to the library. Also in the Options bar is a Search icon to help you find pieces of music.

When you tap the Left Nav button in the Music library, you also see shopping options such as Best Sellers and New Releases. Further down, you find two more options: Settings and Help. The sidebar "Music library settings" tells you about Settings options.

Searching for Music

If you want to find a certain music selection in your library, you can use the Search feature. This feature allows you to search your libraries, the Amazon Store, or the web.

Follow these steps to search for content:

1. **Tap the Search button on the Options bar.**

   The Search field appears.

2. **Tap a tab: Libraries, Stores, or Web (see Figure 7-3).**

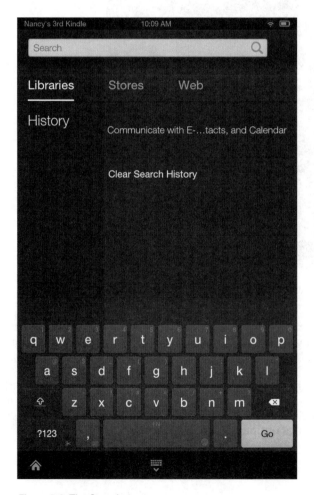

Figure 7-3: The Search screen.

Music library settings

If you tap the Left Nav button and then tap Settings, you see two settings:

✔ **Clear Cache:** This clears any data that has been stored to speed up future music downloads.

✔ **Automatic Downloads:** This setting allows you to choose to automatically download selections to your Kindle Fire HDX whenever you save them to the Amazon Cloud.

---

3. **Tap in the search field and enter the title of a piece of music or a performer.**

4. **Tap Go on the onscreen keyboard.**

   Kindle Fire HDX displays results that match the search term(s).

5. **Tap a result in Music to display music items in your library, the Music store, or the web.**

Uploading Music to the Cloud

One way to add music to your Kindle Fire HDX Music library is by buying it from the Amazon Music Store.

You can also transfer a musical selection or collection stored on your computer (the music you've bought through iTunes, for example) by using the Kindle Fire HDX's micro USB cable. (Read more about this process in Chapter 2.)

In addition, the Amazon Cloud allows you to upload music from your computer; after you upload music, it's available to you through your Kindle Fire HDX Music library.

 Any MP3s you've purchased online from Amazon are automatically stored in the Amazon Cloud. For items you've imported, the first 250 are stored in the Amazon Cloud for free.

Follow these steps to upload music from your computer to the Amazon Cloud:

1. **Go to** `www.amazon.com/cloudplayer` **on your PC or Mac.**

2. **Sign in to your Amazon account.**

   The page shown in Figure 7-4 is displayed.

3. **Click the Import Your Music button.**

   A dialog box appears, asking you to get the Amazon Music Importer.

Figure 7-4: The Amazon Cloud Player is where all your Amazon-purchased music resides.

4. **Click Download Now and follow the instructions that appear to install the Amazon Music Importer.**

   After the Amazon Music Importer has been installed, an Amazon Cloud Player dialog box appears.

5. **Click the Authorize Device button to authorize your computer.**

   You see the dialog box shown in Figure 7-5.

Figure 7-5: Tap into all your music by using the Amazon Music Importer.

6. Click the Start Scan button.

If you'd rather locate the items to import yourself, click the Browse Manually button. The following screen lists the number of songs that were found, and you can click one or more to select them.

7. Click the Import All button.

If you'd rather select the items to import at this point (rather than in the previous step), click the Select Music button instead of the Import All button. If you select Import All, a dialog box appears showing your import progress. You can click the Pause Import button at any time if you want to stop the import process.

After you upload items to your Amazon Cloud library, they're available to Kindle Fire HDX on the Cloud tab of the Music library (see Figure 7-6).

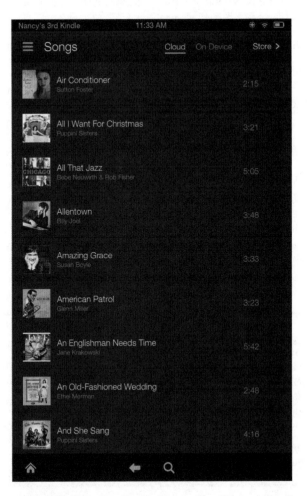

Figure 7-6: Music stored in the Amazon Cloud Player is listed in your Kindle Fire HDX library.

Playing Music

After you have some music available to play (which I explain how to do in the preceding sections), playing that music is an easy task, one that will make fine use of your experience with every other music player you've ever encountered.

Kindle Fire HDX's dual speakers are on the back of the device, so for the best listening experience, turn your device around, and definitely remove any surrounding cover or case from the back side!

Opening and playing a song

First, you have to locate an item to play, and then you can use the playback toolbar to control the playback. Follow these steps to play music from your Music library:

1. **Tap the Music button on the Kindle Fire HDX's Home screen.**

2. **Locate an item you want to play.**

3. **If you are viewing albums, you need to tap to open an album or playlist to view the contents.**

4. **Tap to play the song.**

   If you tap the first song in a group of music selections, such as an album or playlist, Kindle Fire HDX begins to play all selections, starting with the one you tapped.

5. **Use the controls shown in Figure 7-7 to control playback.**

Note: The two items to the left of the Volume button allow you to continuously repeat the selection (the button with the oval consisting of two lines with arrows) and shuffle selections in an album (the *X* formed of two lines with arrows).

Getting sound out by cord or Bluetooth

If you want to use a set of headphones with your Kindle Fire HDX, which can improve the sound and remove extraneous noise, plug a compatible headphone into the headphone jack on the bottom of the device, near the volume buttons.

Alternatively, you can use the Kindle Fire HDX's Bluetooth capability to connect to a Bluetooth headset or speakers. To enable Bluetooth, swipe down from the top of the screen to view Quick Settings, tap Wireless, and then tap Bluetooth. Tap the Bluetooth On button and then tap Pair a Bluetooth Device. In the dialog box that appears, tap the Scan button. Kindle Fire HDX searches for nearby Bluetooth devices.

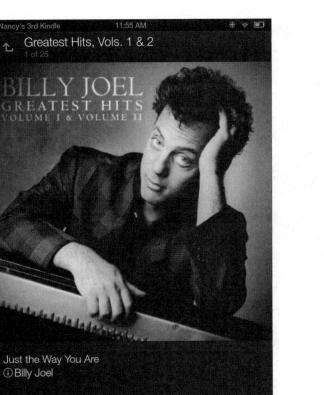

Figure 7-7: Most of these tools are standard playback tools you've probably seen before.

Tap the back arrow on the Options bar to go back to the album or playlist the song belongs to, shown in Figure 7-8. To go back to the Now Playing screen for the song, tap the information bar for the song that appears along the bottom of the screen.

X-Ray for Music

With the most recent Kindle Fire operating system, X-Ray capabilities have been expanded to include Music. X-Ray is a feature that can display information about artists and with music, even song lyrics, as you play content.

Figure 7-8: Tap the currently playing song title at the bottom of the screen to return to it.

Not all music is X-Ray enabled, but if you do own an enabled piece of music, here's how X-Ray works:

1. **From the Home screen, tap Music.**

2. **Locate and tap a song to play it.**

3. **Tap the orange X-Ray Lyrics button, shown in Figure 7-9.**

   The lyrics appear underneath the album image.

4. **Tap the X-Ray Lyrics button again and the lyrics appear full screen over the album picture (see Figure 7-10).**

   You can tap X-Ray Lyrics again to reduce the display of lyrics or tap it twice to remove them from the screen.

5. **Tap the artist's name with an encircled "i" next to it (just above the progress bar).**

   Information about the artist is displayed.

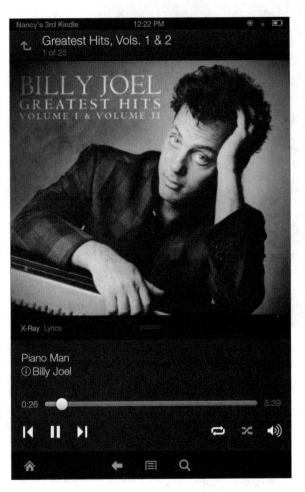

Figure 7-9: X-Ray enabled selections will have an X-Ray Lyrics option.

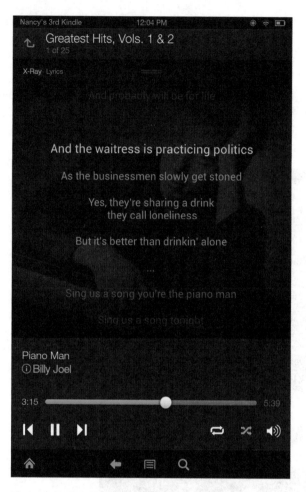

Figure 7-10: Scrolling lyrics help you sing along.

Creating playlists

Playlists allow you to create collections of songs that transcend the boundaries of albums or artists. For example, you might want to create a playlist of songs from a variety of sources for a romantic evening, a dance party, or a mellow road trip.

To create a playlist, follow these steps:

1. Connect to a Wi-Fi network if you aren't already connected.

Creating a playlist requires a Wi-Fi connection because playlists are saved to the Cloud. If you have a 4G model of Kindle Fire HDX, you can do this using your 4G connection.

2. **Tap Music on the Home screen and then tap the Left Nav button.**

3. **Tap Playlists and then tap the Add button (the one with a plus sign on it).**

   The Create New Playlist dialog box appears (see Figure 7-11).

4. **Enter a name for your playlist.**

5. **Tap Save.**

   Kindle Fire HDX displays a screen containing a Search field and a list of songs stored on the device, as shown in Figure 7-12.

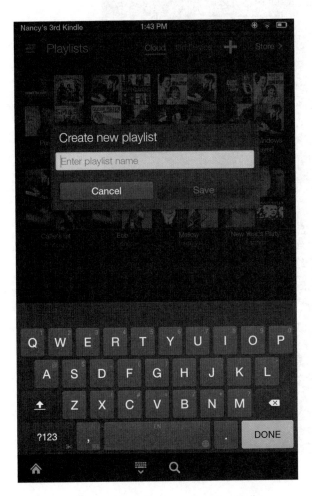

Figure 7-11: Enter a descriptive name for your playlist.

6. Tap the Add Song (+) button to the right of any song to select it.

If you've stored a lot of music and want to find a song without scrolling down the list, enter a song name in the Search field till the list narrows down to display it.

7. Tap Done to save your playlist.

The Playlist is displayed (see Figure 7-13) and includes an Edit button that you can tap to edit the playlist contents.

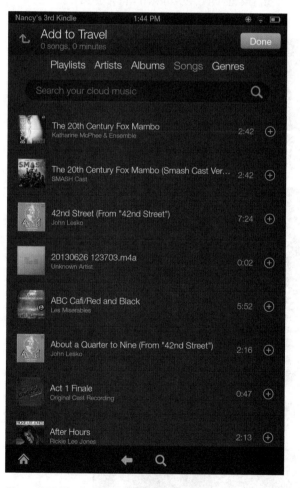

Figure 7-12: The items you buy and download can be stored in playlists.

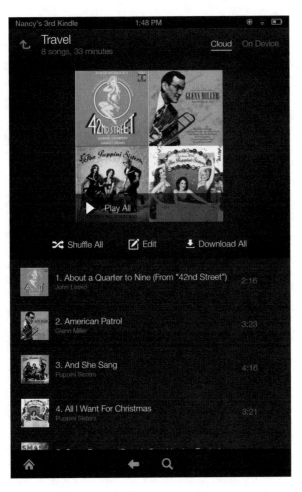

Figure 7-13: A saved playlist.

You can play the newly created playlist by simply tapping the Left Nav button and tapping Playlist. Tap the list you want to play and then tap Play All.

Editing a playlist

After you create a playlist, you can change the name of the list, add more songs, or delete some. To add songs to a playlist, follow these steps:

1. **Tap the Music app on the Home Screen.**

2. **Tap the Left Nav button and then tap Playlists.**

3. **Tap a playlist to display it.**

4. **Tap the Edit button.**

   Songs appear with a Delete (–) symbol next to them; tap this symbol to delete a song.

5. **Tap the Add Songs button and tap the add button next to any song to add it to the playlist.**

6. **Tap the Back button in the Option bar to return to the playlist.**

If you want to rename the playlist, tap the Rename tab in Step 5, enter a new name in the dialog box that appears, and then tap Save.

Playing Video

In This Chapter

▶ Streaming or downloading videos

▶ Poring over your Videos library

▶ Watching movies and TV shows

▶ Getting the facts from X-Ray

*P*laying video, both movies and TV shows, is a great use of Kindle Fire HDX. The device has a bright, crisp screen, can easily be held in one hand, and is capable of streaming video from the Amazon Cloud, making for a typically seamless viewing experience without hogging memory on the tablet itself.

In addition, Amazon offers an amazing selection of video content, including absolutely free Prime Instant Videos (as long as you maintain a Prime account with Amazon beyond the free 30 days that come with the device).

You can discover the ins and outs of buying video content in Chapter 4. In this chapter, I explain how Amazon streams video content from the Cloud to your device, give you a look at the Kindle Fire HDX Videos library, and cover the steps involved in playing a video. In addition, I introduce you to the X-Ray for Video and Music feature that makes use of the Amazon-owned IMDb movie database to provide background info on many videos as you watch and provide an overview of the new Second Screen TV feature.

Streaming versus Downloading

When you tap the Videos button on the Kindle Fire HDX Home screen, you're immediately taken to the Amazon Videos Store (see Figure 8-1), rather than to a library of video titles. (Most of the other buttons along the top, such as

Music or Books, open to your library of content on the device. See Chapter 2 for more about working with libraries of content.) Having Videos, on the other hand, open straight into to the Videos store makes sense because, by design, Kindle Fire HDX is best used to stream videos from the Cloud rather than play them from a library on the device. The device's relatively small memory (16, 32, or 64GB depending on the model you own) can't accommodate a large number of video files, so instead, Amazon makes it easy for you to stream video to the device from the Internet without ever downloading it. If you do have some video content on your device, all you have to do to go to your Videos library after you've opened the Videos app is tap the Library button in the top-right corner.

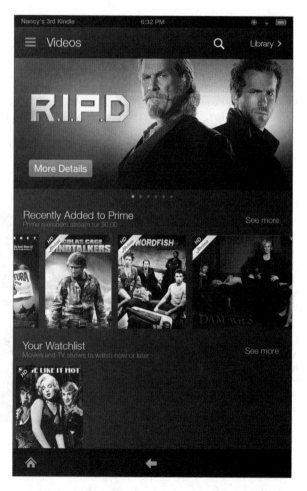

Figure 8-1: The Amazon Videos Store offers thousands of titles.

Swipe upward to scroll down the video content in the Videos store and view categories, including a few categories of Prime Instant Videos (see Figure 8-2), a feature which offers thousands of titles for free with an Amazon Prime account. (If you don't already have an Amazon Prime account, you get one free month of Amazon Prime with your Kindle Fire HDX, after which you can purchase a membership for $79 a year.) You can also purchase or rent other video programs and stream them from the Cloud.

In the Videos store or library, you can tap the Left Nav button to display a list of categories of video content such as New Releases and For the Kids.

Figure 8-2: Browse thousands of free titles in the Prime Instant Videos section of the Videos store.

Amazon's Whispersync technology keeps track of the spot in a video where you stopped watching on any device. You can later resume watching that video at that exact location on Kindle Fire HDX, a PC or Mac, or one of more than 300 compatible TVs, Blu-ray Disc players, or other devices.

You *can* download videos you purchase (you can't download Prime Instant Videos, however), which is useful if you want to watch them away from a Wi-Fi connection. Amazon is the only online streaming video company to offer this feature. It's a good idea to remove them from the device when you're done, to save space.

To delete a video from your device:

1. **Tap Videos and then Library to open your content library.**

2. **Tap the On Device tab.**

   Either the Movies or TV video content displays, depending on which tab you have selected.

3. **Press and hold your finger on the video you want to delete.**

4. **Tap Remove from Device in the menu that appears.**

Looking at Your Videos Library

I'm betting that a lot of you are going to find that viewing video one-on-one on your Kindle Fire HDX is a great way to get your entertainment. The Kindle Fire HDX Videos library may become your favorite destination for buying, viewing, and organizing your video content.

To open the Amazon Videos Store, tap Videos on your Kindle Fire HDX Home screen (refer to Figure 8-1).

The store shows several video categories in rows running down the screen, such as Recently Added, Movies, Television, or Prime Instant Videos as well as Your Watchlist. I tell you more about Watchlist in a bit.

Navigating categories

When you see a category that you want to explore, tap the words See More to the right of the category name (refer to Figure 8-2), and that category's contents are displayed.

For example, to get around in the Popular Movies on Prime Instant Videos category, follow these steps:

1. **Tap See More for the Popular Movies on Prime Instant Videos category.**

   A screen appears, with a down-arrow next to the words "Popular Movies, Prime" near the top left of the screen.

2. **Tap the down-arrow to open a drop-down list.**

   Categories such as Popular Movies, Recently Added, Editor's Picks, For the Kids, and more appear in the list (see Figure 8-3). When you tap any of these categories, additional items related to that category appear on the list to help you narrow down your search for content.

The categories may change over time, but the basic process of locating a selection and displaying its details should stay the same.

When you have displayed the list in Step 2 in the preceding list, you see two tabs: Categories and Filter. Categories lists additional categories of content, whereas Filter offers the option of Prime-only content, Closed Captions for content that offers this feature, and X-Ray for content that takes advantage of the X-Ray feature for displaying information about cast members.

Figure 8-3: See what editors choose as their favorite videos in the Videos store.

Creating Your Watchlist

Watchlist is a way to make note of items you may want to watch in the future. When you add videos to your watchlist, you'll find them in two categories: Movies and TV. Here's how to add any video to your Watchlist:

1. **In the Amazon Videos Store, tap and hold the video.**

   A menu appears.

2. **Tap Add to Watchlist.**

Tap any video in the various lists to get more details about it.

Searching for and filtering content

When you tap the Search button in the store, the Kindle Fire HDX keyboard pops up, and you can enter search criteria such as an actor's name or show's name.

Tap the Library button to go to your Videos library (see Figure 8-4). The library sports two tabs listing the following:

✔ All your videos stored in the Cloud

✔ Videos you've purchased that you have downloaded to the device

The tab that's orange is the active tab.

Figure 8-4: The Kindle Fire HDX Videos library stored in the Amazon Cloud.

In addition to the Cloud and Device tabs, there are two tabs for filtering content: by Movies or TV programs. You can tap the Search button in the Options bar (on the right side of the screen when the Kindle Fire HDX is in landscape orientation and at the bottom of the screen in portrait orientation) to search for a particular video.

Downloaded video content is listed chronologically by the date you downloaded it.

Tap the Left Nav button to display useful categories of content such as New Releases and Most Popular, as well as Settings and Help options. (Keep swiping to get to the categories near the bottom.)

You can tap the Left Nav button and then tap For the Kids in any category to view videos appropriate for younger viewers.

Setting video quality

In Settings, you can choose settings for HD (high definition) and SD (standard definition and therefore lower quality than HD) download quality (see Figure 8-5). If you set a quality preference, Kindle Fire won't ask you for your preference before downloading high-definition or standard-definition videos. Though it's a good idea to be selective about downloading HD videos because they can take up a lot of memory, you may grow tired of seeing the message every time you download your new favorite flick.

Opening and Playing a Video

Playing a video is a simple process. If the video has been downloaded to your device, open your library (tap Videos and then tap the Library button), locate the video (using methods described in the preceding section), and then tap the video to play it. If you've played the video before, you may have to tap a Resume, Start Over, or Download button to get it going again (see Figure 8-6).

If you're streaming a video that's stored in the Cloud, follow these steps:

1. **On the Kindle Fire HDX's Home screen, tap Videos.**

2. **Tap the Library button in the top-right corner of the screen.**

3. **Tap the Cloud tab.**

   Videos you've rented (whose rental period hasn't expired) or purchased are displayed.

4. **Tap an item to open it.**

If it's a TV show, you see episodes listed (see Figure 8-7). Tap one to open it or tap the Buy button to buy an entire season. If it's a movie, at this point you see a description of the movie and the option of watching it or downloading it (see Figure 8-8).

5. **Tap the Watch Now button.**

The playback controls appear.

6. **If you've already watched part of the video, tap the Resume button (see Figure 8-6).**

Figure 8-5: Check out options for downloading HD and SD videos here.

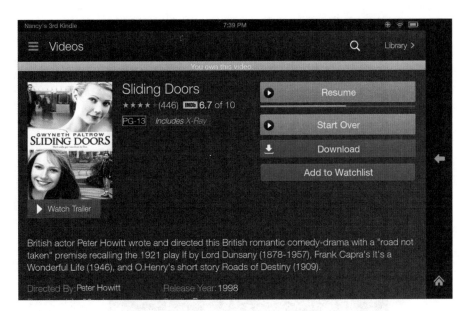

Figure 8-6: Start again or resume where you left off.

If you'd rather see a video you've previously watched from its start, tap the Start Over button.

The video appears full screen with playback controls along the bottom (see Figure 8-9). The title of the Movie appears at the bottom of the screen.

Note that the Kindle Fire HDX screen provides an extra-wide viewing angle. This means that you and those watching with you (well, maybe one person watching with you — it does have a 7-inch or 8.9-inch screen, after all) can see the content from the side as well as from straight on.

The familiar playback tools available here include

- Play
- Pause
- A progress bar
- A volume slider
- A button that shows "10" in a circle; tapping this button moves you ten seconds back in the video
- A Full Screen button
- In the case of TV shows, a Next Episode button

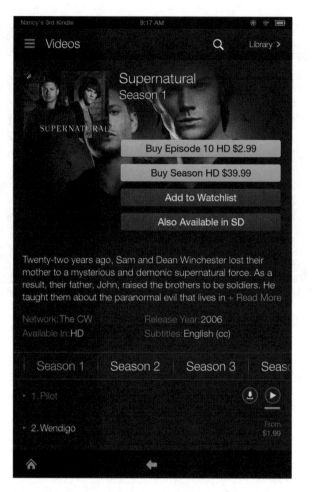

Figure 8-7: The episode list for a popular TV show.

There's also a Back button in the Options bar that you can tap to stop play-back and return to the Videos store.

When you display a video's details in the Amazon Videos Store, you can scroll down and read IMDb movie database trivia and information about the cast and reviews and ratings. See the later section, "Using X-Ray for Video and Movies," for more about this feature.

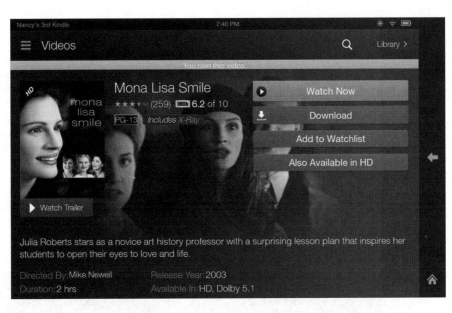

Figure 8-8: A new movie to watch!

Figure 8-9: Move playback controls on Kindle Fire HDX.

Using Second Screen to Fling a Movie to Your TV

A few months after the launch of Kindle Fire HDX, a new feature called Second Screen will be available. Second Screen, which uses a technology called Miracast, allows you to "fling" movies and TV shows to your television. Second Screen streams the content to your TV and frees up your Kindle Fire to use its other apps and features as you wish. You can also use your Kindle Fire to control playback and display X-Ray information about the movie or show you're watching.

When it first appears, Second Screen will be available for PlayStation 3 and Samsung televisions, but other Miracast-enabled devices will no doubt be added in the future.

Using X-Ray for Video and Music

When Kindle Fire HD arrived, so did the X-Ray feature. This feature works with some books, music, and movies to give you access to facts about what you're reading, listening to, or watching. This feature is based in part on the IMDb database of movie trivia, which Amazon, coincidentally, owns. X-Ray has been made much more robust with the arrival of Fire OS 3.0 and Kindle Fire HDX and now includes coverage of TV shows, though at this point it works only with selected content. (If you want to try it, play an episode of Downton Abbey, free with your Prime Instant Video account.)

In the case of movies, the X-Ray feature provides information about the cast (see Figure 8-10), and if you tap a particular cast member, you get details about that person's career and other movies he or she has appeared in (Figure 8-11).

Figure 8-10: Find out more about the cast while watching the movie.

If you're playing music you bought from Amazon, with certain selections you can get both information about artists, such as what other artists they've worked with, and lyrics to some songs.

Figure 8-11: If you like the star, look for other movies featuring her here.

To display X-Ray information, follow these steps:

1. **Tap the screen when an X-Ray enabled movie or TV show is playing.**

   The cast list appears along the left of the screen.

2. **Tap the View All button to see the entire cast list.**

3. **Tap a cast member.**

   Details like those shown in Figure 8-11 appear.

9

Going Social

In This Chapter

▶ Working with the Contacts app

▶ Utilizing integrated Facebook and Twitter features

▶ Conducting video calls with Skype

Kindle Fire HDX isn't just about reading books, watching movies, and playing music. There are several ways in which you can use the device to interact and communicate with others.

In this chapter, I help you explore how Kindle Fire HDX helps you keep in touch with people using the pre-installed Contacts app. I also explain how Kindle Fire HDX integrates with Facebook and Twitter. Finally, I tell you all about using the Skype app and the new Kindle Fire HDX cameras and microphones to make video calls over the Internet.

Managing Contacts

The Contacts app pre-installed on Kindle Fire HDX is a basic but useful contact management tool. You can enter or import contact information, sort that information by several criteria, and use Contacts to address e-mails.

You can find Contacts by tapping its app on the Kindle Fire grid at the bottom of the Home screen. Tap the Contacts app to display its main screen, as shown in Figure 9-1.

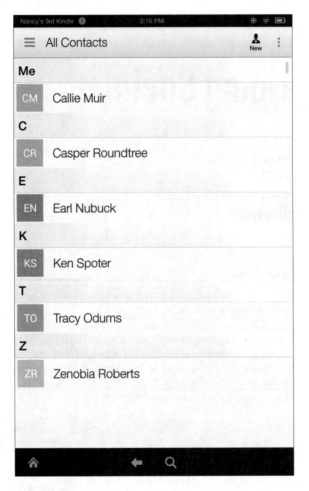

Figure 9-1: The Contacts app main screen with several contacts entered.

Importing contacts

If you have associated an e-mail account with your Kindle Fire HDX, you can import all contacts from that account instead of entering each contact's information individually. (See Chapter 5 for more about setting up an e-mail provider account to sync with your Kindle Fire HDX.)

After you have set up an associated e-mail account, when you first open Contacts and tap the New button near the top-right corner, you get a message like that shown in Figure 9-2. Tap the account from which you want to import contacts. Your contacts are imported.

Figure 9-2: Synchronize to import contacts from your e-mail account.

Note that you may see a message offering you the option to turn off the feature that backs your contacts up to the Cloud. Because contacts from your e-mail account are saved to Amazon Cloud and then, therefore, available to your Kindle Fire, you need to leave the feature turned on to complete the import.

If you want to create a new account, you can tap the Add New Account button at this point, enter another e-mail address, and tap Next. Enter a password and tap Next. Kindle Fire syncs with the account.

Creating new contacts

It's data entry time! Importing contacts (see the preceding section) is a nice shortcut, but you can also add contacts to your Amazon account or an e-mail account you've set up on Kindle Fire from the device itself.

To create a new contact, follow these steps:

1. **Tap the Contact app on the Carousel or in the Apps library to open it and then tap the New button in the upper-right corner to create a new contact.**

   The first time you do this, you may see a dialog box that lists Amazon and any e-mail accounts you've set up with an Add New Account button. After you've added an account, you'll see a Contacts screen (see Figure 9-3) that contains fields including First Name, Last Name, Phone, and so on. Tap the top field to select whether to add the contact to your Amazon Cloud account or an e-mail account.

Figure 9-3: The Contact form.

2. **Tap in a field such as First Name and enter text.**

   The onscreen keyboard appears when you tap in a field.

3. **When you're done entering text in one field, tap the Next button on the onscreen keyboard to go to the next field.**

   You have to scroll to the bottom if you want to enter detailed address information. You can tap Add More Fields at the bottom of the form to choose additional information fields to include.

4. **Tap the Photo icon at the top of the form and then tap Add Photo to add a photo.**

   Options appear for selecting photos, as shown in Figure 9-4.

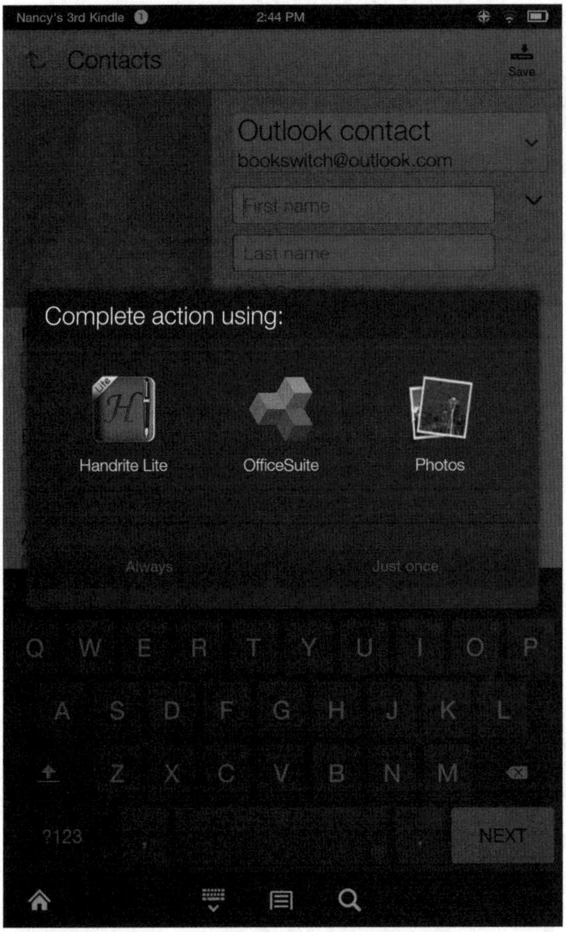

Figure 9-4: Choose the Photos option.

5. **Tap a photo source such as Photos to open it, double-tap to open a photo album; then tap a photo to add it to the contact record.**

6. **Tap Save.**

The contact information displays as shown in Figure 9-5.

To edit the contact, tap the Edit button. To delete the contact, tap the Delete button. To display all contacts, tap the All button.

Figure 9-5: A contact record with photo included.

Viewing and organizing contacts

You can use settings to control how your contacts are organized and even save contacts to a list of Favorites in the Contacts app.

To sort your contacts, follow these steps:

1. **On the bar across the top of the Contacts list, tap the Left Nav button and then tap Settings.**

   The E-Mail, Contacts, and Calendar settings appear.

2. **Tap Contacts General Settings.**

3. **Tap Sort Order of Contact Name to display the options shown in Figure 9-6.**

4. **Tap to sort by first name or last name.**

You can also choose to view contacts in the Favorites area of the Home screen. To add a contact to Favorites, follow these steps:

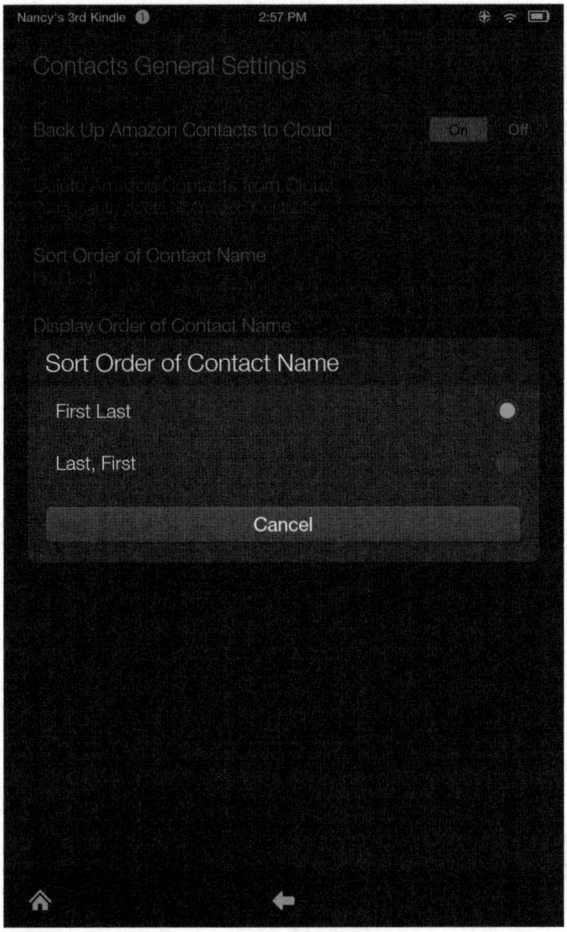

Figure 9-6: Choose from these basic sorting options.

1. **Tap Contacts in the Favorites grid on the Home screen.**

   The Contacts app opens.

2. **Tap the contact name you want to make a favorite.**

3. **Tap the star that appears next to the contact's name, as shown in Figure 9-7.**

   The star turns orange, indicating that this is a favorite.

4. **Tap the Back arrow in the Options bar to display all contacts.**

   You see a circled orange star in the initials (or photo, if you have added a photo for the contact) to the left of the contact name.

Figure 9-7: Tap the star to place a contact into Favorites.

Using Integrated Facebook and Twitter

If you want to work with your Facebook and Twitter accounts from your Kindle Fire HDX, you can download those free apps from the Amazon Appstore. In order to share items via Facebook and Twitter, you can use integrated tools in Kindle Fire HDX itself. You can share photos, notes, and highlights from books, YouTube videos, and more.

For example, if you're reading a book in your library, you can tap the screen to display tools and then tap the Share button at the top of the screen. This offers you the options shown in Figure 9-8 to share your notes and highlights via Facebook or Twitter.

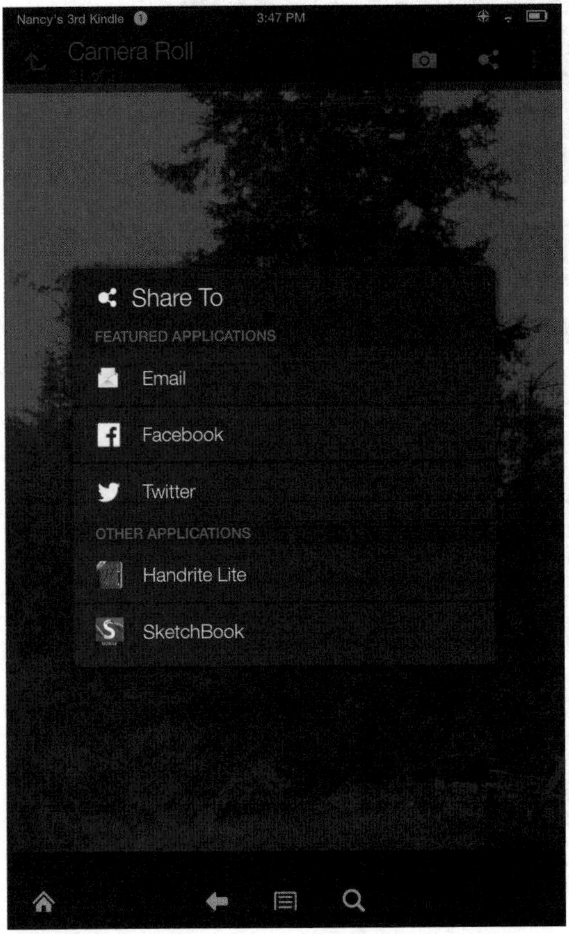

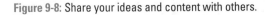

Figure 9-8: Share your ideas and content with others.

To share via Facebook or Twitter, just tap one of those options (refer to Figure 9-8), and a screen like the one shown in Figure 9-9 appears. Enter your account information and then tap Connect to sign in to your account and post your notes and highlights to your Facebook page or Twitter account.

You can also share photos by displaying one in the Photos app and then tapping the Share To button. Tap Email, Facebook, or Twitter and use the form that appears (see Figure 9-10) to enter a message or sign in to your account to share the photo.

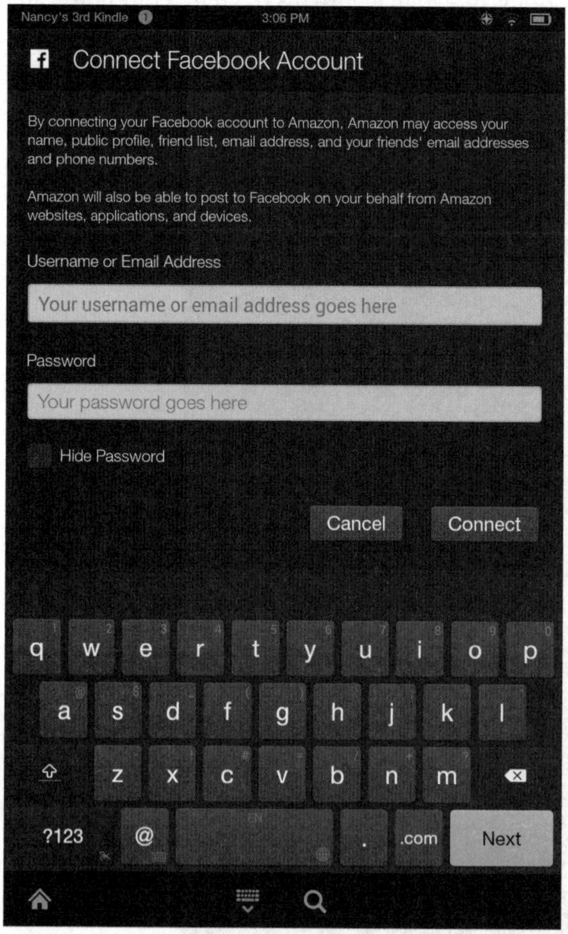

Figure 9-9: Share by signing in to your Facebook or Twitter account.

Figure 9-10: Share photos and more with friends on Facebook.

Making Calls with Skype

With Kindle Fire HDX comes a camera (front facing and rear facing on the 8.9" model, and front facing only on the 7") and microphone. What they allow you to do is to make regular phone calls or video calls to others using the popular Skype app, for which you may already have an account. The Skype app for Kindle Fire HDX is free, but you will have to download it from the Amazon Appstore (see Chapter 4 for more about getting apps).

Skype has recently reinvented its app for Android in version 4.4, so if you've used Skype before, you'll see a rather new interface when you download the free app for Kindle Fire HDX.

Conversations are given more emphasis, with recent calls and chats front and center. Video call quality is improved — which, together with the Kindle Fire HDX's crisp resolution on 7" models and even better resolution on 8.9" models makes for some very clear HD (high definition) video indeed.

When you have downloaded the Skype app, tap Apps from the Home Screen and then follow these steps:

1. **Tap the Skype app to open it. On the Welcome to Skype screen, you may be asked to tap Continue and then tap Accept on the following screen to accept terms and conditions.**

2. **Enter your Skype Name and Password.**

   If you've never created a Skype account, tap the Create an Account button at this point and enter your name, Skype Name, password, e-mail address, and phone number to create your Skype account.

3. **Tap the Sign In button and, on the following screen, tap Continue.**

   On the screen that appears (see Figure 9-11), you should tap the Echo/ Sound Test button in the People section and then tap the Call button (shaped like a phone handset) to verify that your connection is set up properly.

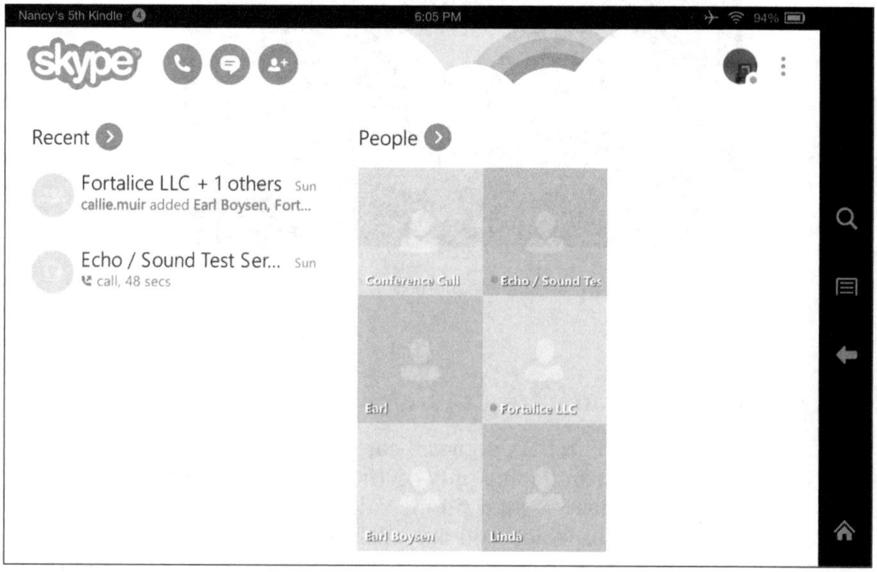

Figure 9-11: The main Skype screen offers a way to test your connection.

4. **At this point, you choose one of these options:**

- **People:** This area displays a list of contacts you've saved to your Skype contacts. Tap one, and on the screen that appears, tap the Call button, as shown in Figure 9-12) to place a call.

- **Add:** Tap the Add button, the rightmost button of the three buttons near the top-left corner of the screen; then tap Add People or Add Number. Enter a name or number and the Skype app searches for a matching Skype user. When it returns information, tap a person, and then on the following screen, tap Add to Contacts. This provides you with an automated message telling the person that you want to add him or her to your Skype contacts. Tap Send to send the message. When the person responds positively, he or she is added to your Skype contacts.

- **Call:** Tap the Call button, which is the leftmost button in the row of three buttons on the top of the Skype home screen, and then enter a phone number on the onscreen keypad that appears, as shown in Figure 9-13.

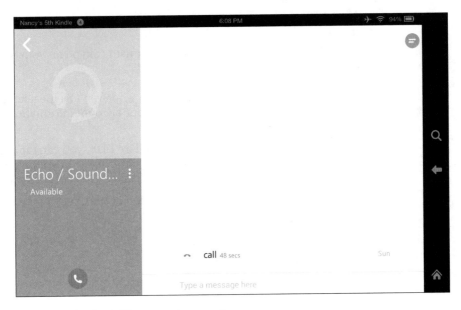

Figure 9-12: Tap the Call button to place a call.

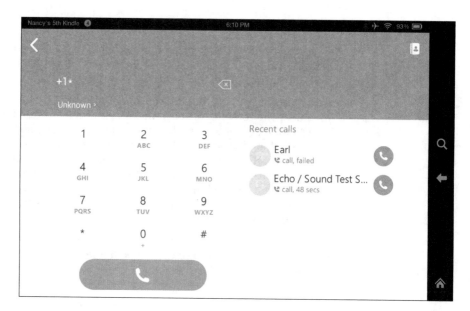

Figure 9-13: Enter any number here and place your call.

Here are a few more tips to remember about using Skype on your Kindle Fire HDX:

- ✔ You need to have credits to call people who aren't Skype users. Go to www.skype.com and sign in with your account information to buy credits.

- ✔ From the Skype main screen on Kindle Fire HDX, you can tap the Profile button and enter a message that's shared with any of your contacts that you select, such as the phone number you use to accept Skype calls.

- ✔ You can tap an item in the Recent section of the Skype home screen to call someone you recently called again.

- ✔ Tap the photo or photo placeholder to the left of the Menu button (it looks like three vertical dots) in the top-right corner of the Skype app main screen to display your profile, edit it, and set up payment options, or choose settings that tell people you're either available or invisible (at least to Skype callers).

- ✔ You can tap the Menu button and then tap the Settings option to access settings for receiving incoming calls, syncing contacts, signing in automatically, and so on, as shown in Figure 9-14.

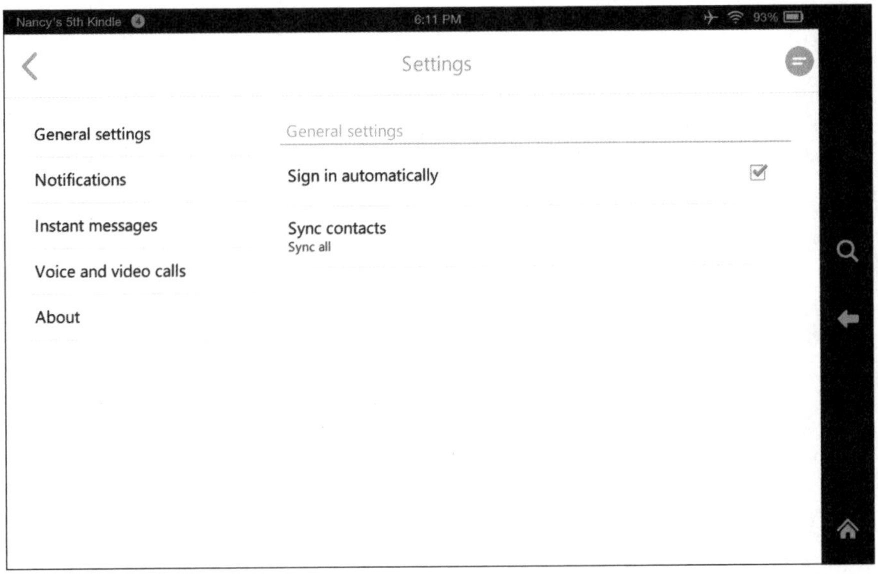

Figure 9-14: You can control your incoming and outgoing call experience with these settings.

10

Getting Productive with Kindle Fire HDX

In This Chapter

▶ Understanding how Kindle Fire HDX treats documents

▶ Working with Calendar

▶ Taking photos and videos

▶ Working with the built-in OfficeSuite

*K*indle Fire HDX isn't just about watching movies and playing music. There are several ways in which you can use the device to get your work done and share documents and images with others.

In this chapter, I help you explore how Kindle Fire HDX helps you view and share documents. The new pre-installed Calendar app is useful for keeping on schedule, and it's covered in this chapter.

New with Fire OS 3.0 and Kindle Fire HDX are several handy features. You can now print documents and photos to a wireless printer. In addition, the OfficeSuite Pro is now built in, allowing you to view, create, and edit documents. With improved cameras (front and rear on the 8.9-inch model), you can take both still photos and videos, and then manage your photos with the Photos app and Amazon Cloud.

And finally, I show you the easy-to-use features that make the free New Oxford American Dictionary a very useful tool for the writer in you.

Understanding Kindle Docs

One of the items you see across the top of your Kindle Fire HDX Home screen is the Docs library (see Figure 10-1). Documents will be stored in the Docs library, to which this button provides access, and if you've viewed them recently, they will also be available on the Carousel. You can also save docs to the Favorites grid on the bottom of the Home screen (see Chapter 2 for more about Favorites).

In the following sections, you can discover how docs get onto your Kindle Fire HDX and how you can view and share them. I also provide some advice about using productivity software on Kindle Fire HDX to get your work done.

Figure 10-1: Tap the Docs button to open the Docs library.

Getting Docs onto Kindle Fire HDX

Documents help you communicate information in forms ranging from newsletters to memos and garage sale flyers to meeting agendas. The ability to create, add, and edit documents on your Kindle Fire makes it a very portable and useful tool.

Grabbing docs from your computer

To get a doc onto your Kindle Fire HDX, you can *sideload* (transfer) it from your PC or Mac by using the micro USB cable that comes with Kindle Fire HDX. Once connected, you can simply click and drag documents onto your Kindle Fire device.

To sideload docs to your Kindle Fire HDX, grab the micro USB cable that came with Kindle Fire HDX and then follow these steps:

1. **Attach the micro USB end of the cable to your Kindle Fire HDX.**

2. **Attach the USB end of the cable to your computer.**

   Your Kindle Fire HDX will appear as a drive in Windows Explorer on a Windows computer or the Mac Finder on a Mac (see Figure 10-2).

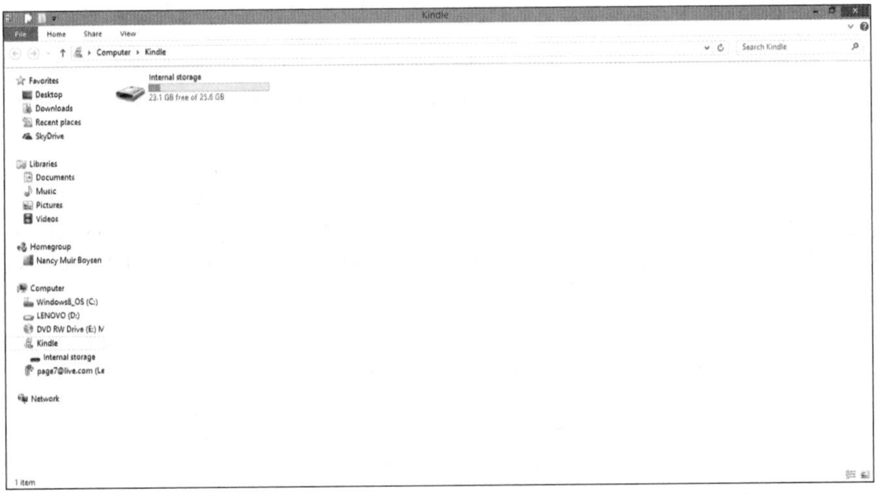

Figure 10-2: Options for opening up content of Kindle Fire HDX.

3. **Click the appropriate choice to open and view files on the drive that appears (see Figure 10-3).**

4. **Double-click the Internal Storage folder and then click and drag files from your hard drive to the Docs folder in the Kindle Fire HDX window.**

You can also copy and paste documents from one drive to the other. Drag documents to the Documents folder, pictures to the Photos folder, audio files to the Music folder, and so on.

5. **Disconnect your Kindle Fire HDX from your computer.**

You can now unplug the micro USB cord from your Kindle Fire HDX and computer.

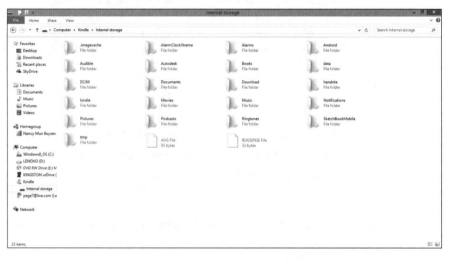

Figure 10-3: Your Kindle Fire HDX appears like an external drive on your computer when attached using a micro USB cable.

Docs that you sideload are only stored on your Kindle Fire HDX, not backed up to the Amazon Cloud. If you want to back up changed versions of these documents, use the micro USB cable to copy them back to your computer.

Sending docs by e-mail

You can also e-mail a document to yourself at your Kindle e-mail address. (Locate this address by swiping down to display Quick Settings and then tapping Settings⇨My Account. Your address appears under your name in the top-left corner.)

Syncing with the Cloud

If you like, you can sync all your PC or Mac documents with your Amazon Cloud Drive, and they will then be available on your Kindle Fire. Here's the process to follow to sync documents:

1. **Tap Docs on the Home screen.**

The Docs library appears (see Figure 10-4).

2. **Tap Sync.**

3. **Tap Email Me Install Links.**

4. **On your computer, open the e-mail from Amazon; then click Download the Cloud Drive App and follow instructions to install the app on your computer.**

5. **On the Cloud Drive window that appears, click Next to proceed; then enter your Amazon account name and password.**

6. **On the following screen, click Create My Cloud Drive Folder.**

   Your Cloud Drive appears as a folder on your computer.

7. **Drag files into the Cloud Drive folder.**

   These files are now available to you on your Kindle Fire.

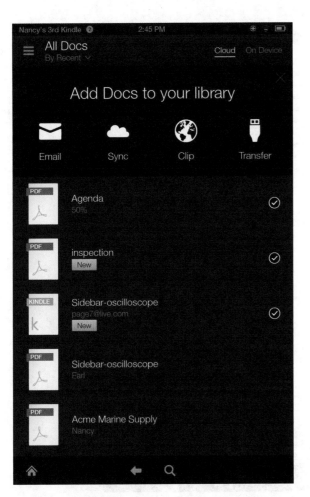

Figure 10-4: Use the Add Docs to Your Library buttons for information on how to get docs into Kindle Fire.

On the Docs screen, you can also tap Clips, e-mail yourself install links to your computer, download the Send to Kindle for Google Chrome and Mozilla Firefox app, and then use the Clips feature in those browsers to save web clips, blog posts, and articles to your Kindle Fire.

Understanding Document File Formats

Documents come in different formats. Some formats come from the originating software, such as Microsoft Word. Other formats can be opened by a variety of software programs, such as RTF documents that can be opened by any word processor program. In Kindle Fire HDX, supported document formats include TXT, Microsoft Word DOCX (see Figure 10-5), HTML, RTF, or PDF (see Figure 10-6), as well as Amazon's Mobi or ASW formats. Some documents will be converted to one of these Amazon formats automatically.

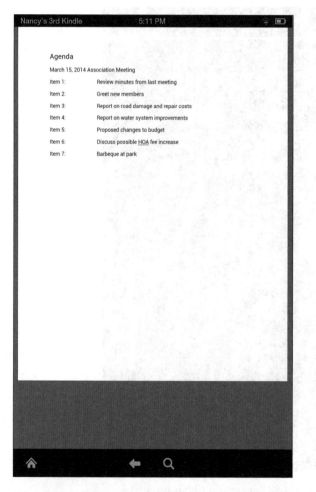

Figure 10-5: A Word document displayed on Kindle Fire HDX.

Acme Marine Supply

1234 Spring Street

Lost Harbor, WA 98838

May 23, 2013

To Whom It May Concern:

Arlene Smith was an employee of our company from June 2010 to April 2013. In her duties Arlene was a
fine employee who was diligent and hard working.

Arlene asked us to write a letter of recommendation to your school. We consider her to be of very good
character, very intelligent and responsible, and she would be an asset to your student body. Please
contact us if you would like any further information about her.

Sincerely,

John Randall

Store Manager

360 555-0099

Figure 10-6: A PDF document displayed on Kindle Fire HDX.

You can also get a variety of common graphic file formats onto Kindle
Fire HDX, and those graphic files will be stored in your Photos app.
Kindle Fire HDX even supports compressed (Zip) file formats and automati-
cally unzips them when they're transferred to your device via e-mail.

Working with Docs

Once you have a document on your Kindle Fire, you'll want to work with
it, opening the doc, printing it, or e-mailing it to others. Those tasks are
covered here.

Opening docs

After you put a doc onto your Kindle Fire HDX, you can view the document
by following these steps:

1. **Tap the Docs button on the Kindle Fire HDX Home screen to open the Docs library.**

   Alternatively, you can locate recently viewed docs on the Carousel and docs you've saved to Favorites in the Favorites grid on the Home screen.

2. **When the library opens (see Figure 10-7), tap Cloud or On Device to see the library contents.**

3. **Tap the Sort button (typically, it reads All Docs) and choose how you'd like the docs in your library to be sorted.**

   You can choose one of three categories: By Name, By Type, or By Recent. If you are looking at docs in your Amazon Cloud Drive account, you can also view them By Folder; you can create folders from the Amazon Cloud Drive site.

Figure 10-7: The Docs library with the Sort button at top left.

4. When you find the document you want to view, tap it to open it.

At this point in time, you can view documents and even edit ones that are compatible with OfficeSuite Pro, such as Word, Excel, and PowerPoint.

To search for a document, tap the Search button in the Options bar and type a document name in the Search field. Tap a tab to search from among Libraries, Stores, or Web. When you've entered the search term, tap Go on the onscreen keyboard.

E-mailing docs

When you have a doc on your Kindle Fire HDX, you can view it as well as share it with others as an e-mail attachment. Follow these steps to attach a doc to an e-mail message:

1. Swipe upward to scroll down to the Favorites grid on the Home screen.

A list of favorite installed apps appears. If you've removed the E-mail app from your Favorites, look for it by tapping the Apps library.

2. Tap the E-mail app.

The E-mail app opens.

3. If necessary, tap your Inbox to display it and then tap the New button (see Figure 10-8).

A blank e-mail form appears, as shown in Figure 10-9.

4. Enter an e-mail address in the To field, a subject, and a message.

5. Tap the Menu button in the top-right corner (the button with three vertical dots on it).

A menu appears (see Figure 10-10).

6. Tap Attach File.

7. Choose to attach an item from the OfficeSuite folder.

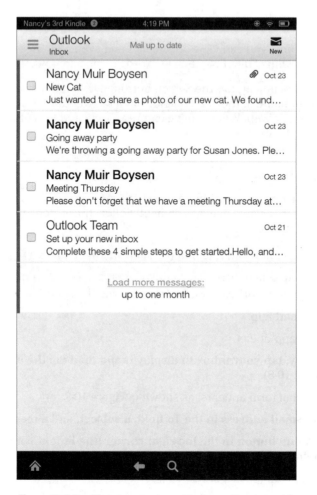

Figure 10-8: Tap New to get going with composing an e-mail.

8. Tap a folder such as Recent Files or My Documents and then tap the document you want to send.

You return to the e-mail form with the document attached.

9. Tap Send.

Your document goes on its way, attached to your e-mail.

Figure 10-9: A blank form waiting for you to enter an e-mail address, subject, and message.

Printing docs: Coming soon

At the time of this writing, the feature for printing to wireless printers wasn't yet available, but here's what I know about it.

When this feature becomes available, you will be able to print the following items from your Kindle Fire to a wireless printer:

- ✔ Documents including spreadsheets, word processor documents, and presentations
- ✔ E-mails
- ✔ Photos

Figure 10-10: Attaching a doc to an e-mail message.

At the time of writing, when you choose a print command, for example from an OfficeSuite app, you are offered the choices to Print with Network Printer or use Google Cloud Print. A new option, Print to Wireless Printer, should appear when this feature is available.

You can check for updates on this feature at www.dummies.com/extras/kindlefirehdx.

Working with OfficeSuite Pro

If you want to do more than view documents on your Kindle Fire HDX, consider using the built-in app called OfficeSuite Pro (see Figure 10-11). This productivity suite for Android gives you the ability to create, view, and edit word processor, spreadsheet, and presentation files. The popular Microsoft Office suite products Word, Excel, and PowerPoint are supported in this app.

See Chapter 11 for a list of great apps you can get to flesh out your Kindle Fire HDX functionality, such as calculator and note-taking apps.

Opening a document in OfficeSuite Pro

When you open OfficeSuite Pro, you have access to the three apps contained in it (refer to Figure 10-10 to view the opening screen).

To open a new, blank document, tap any of the three apps: Document, Spreadsheet, or Presentation.

To open an existing document, tap Recent Files, My Documents, Internal Storage, or Remote Files to locate a file and then tap the one you want to open. Here's what these folders contain:

- My Documents contains files from your Docs library.

- Internal Storage provides access to all your Kindle Fire folders, such as Music and Books.

- Remote Files lets you add a remote online file-sharing site account such as Dropbox and SkyDrive and access files stored on them.

Using editing tools

Although the scope of this book doesn't allow for an in-depth tutorial on using all the formatting tools offered by the various OfficeSuite Pro apps, I can give you an overview. When you have a document open in an app, tools run along the bottom of the screen (see Figure 10-12). Here's a quick rundown on some of the tools you can use to format selected text:

Figure 10-11: The various pieces of OfficeSuite are available from this opening page.

- **Font:** Tap the far-left tool with double *A*'s and you can set font style such as Heading or Quote, font family such as Calibri, and font size.

- **Bold/Italic/Underline:** This popular trio of text formatting tools help you emphasize certain text in your doc.

- **Font Alignment:** Tap any of three tools to align text left, centered, or right.

- **Lists:** Use the Bullet List or Number List buttons to style selected text in lists.

- **Indent:** You can indent or outdent text relative to the doc margins.

There are also buttons for a quick spell check and printing on this toolbar.

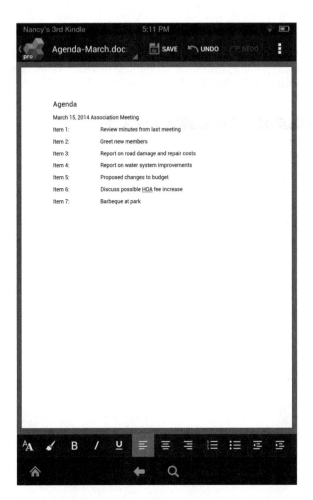

Figure 10-12: An assortment of pretty sophisticated editing tools is available to you in OfficeSuite Pro.

Staying on Time with Calendar

The pre-installed Calendar app offers a simple calendar interface, which you can display by day, week, or month. The Calendar app allows you to sync with calendars from your e-mail account and then view and edit events and create new events.

Calendar views

Before you can use many of Calendar's features, you have to sync it with a calendar account, typically through your e-mail provider. When you first open Calendar, you see the blank calendar shown in Figure 10-13.

Figure 10-13: The Calendar app can be coordinated with your e-mail account calendar.

Tap the word Calendar to display a menu from which you can choose to display the calendar by Day, Week, or Month, or to display a List of events.

To move to other dates, use the buttons along the bottom of the screen (refer to Figure 10-13). In Day view, these buttons will be dates just before and after the currently displayed day; in Week view, the buttons will be labeled for weeks just before and after the current week; and in Month view, you tap a button to display another month.

Syncing with a calendar account

A quick way to coordinate all your events on your e-mail calendar is to sync it with your Kindle Fire Calendar app. Follow these steps to sync your calendars and bring your e-mail events over to the Calendar app and vice versa:

1. **Tap the Left Nav button.**

   A list of calendar options appears. Note that the options presented here will vary based on your e-mail account features and whether you've set up other accounts such as Facebook.

2. **Tap My Calendar (or the name of your specific e-mail account calendar) to sync with your e-mail account calendar.**

If you've set up a Facebook account on your Kindle Fire, you will see a Birthday Calendar in the Navigation menu. Tap this option to add birthdays from friends in your Facebook account, or tap U.S. Holidays to add those dates.

Adding a new event

Besides getting events from your e-mail calendar, you can also add individual events in your Calendar app. When you create an event in your Calendar app, it is copied to your e-mail application's calendar, and you receive an e-mail about the event in your e-mail Inbox.

Here are the steps to add an event:

1. **Tap the Menu button (refer to Figure 10-13) and then tap the New Event option in the menu that appears.**

2. **In the screen shown in Figure 10-14, add the details of your event, such as title, location, start and end time, and so on.**

   If you want to have the event repeat (say, every Tuesday), tap the Repeat drop-down list and choose an interval; if you want a reminder in Notifications, tap Reminders and choose how far ahead of the event the reminder should appear.

3. **Tap Save to save the event.**

To edit an event, simply tap to open it, tap the Menu button and then tap Edit on the menu that appears.

Taking and Viewing Photos and Video

Kindle Fire HDX has a still and video camera built in so that you can take pictures and videos. There's also a pre-installed Photos app for all you photography lovers. With improved features in Kindle Fire HDX, Photos allows you to view and do minor edits to photos.

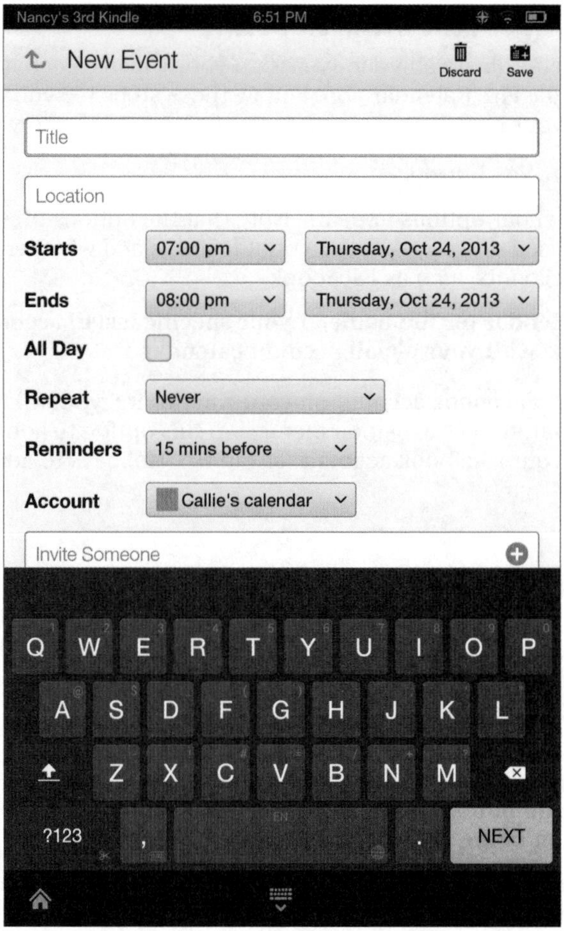

Figure 10-14: Add your event details.

Taking photos

The 7-inch and 8.9-inch Kindle Fire HDX models have front-facing cameras, and the 8.9-inch model has both a front- and rear-facing camera (handy for those Skype calls when you want to show the other person what you're looking at.

You can use your front-facing camera on either model to take both still photos and videos using the Camera app. To take a photo, follow these steps:

1. **On the Home screen, scroll down to the Favorites grid and tap the Camera app.**

   The Camera opens.

2. **Tap the Camera/Video button. (In portrait orientation, this appears on the top-left corner; in landscape, it's on the left side of the screen about a third of the way down.)**

To set this app to take still photos, make sure the Camera symbol is the larger of the two; if it isn't, tap the button again (see Figure 10-15).

4. **Hold the Kindle Fire and move it around until you see the image you want to capture.**

5. **Tap the Capture button (it's the circular one that looks like a little camera aperture).**

   Your picture is taken and appears as a thumbnail above the Capture button. You can tap the picture thumbnail to view it in your camera roll.

If you have an 8.9-inch model with a rear-facing camera, first tap the Front/Rear button (the bottom of the two buttons on the left side of the camera screen), and you can then use the image on your screen to locate the shot you want to take and tap the Capture button.

Figure 10-15: Set the Camera to still photos and then tap Capture to get your photo.

Recording video

Are your friend and you trying parasailing for the first time? Is it your daughter's 16th birthday? Do you want to capture midnight at your New Year's Eve party? You'll be happy to hear that you can use your Kindle Fire HDX to capture and play back video.

To capture a video, follow these steps:

1. **On the Home screen, swipe upward to scroll down to the Favorites grid and tap the Camera app.**

   The Camera opens.

2. **Tap the Camera/Video button. (In portrait orientation, this appears on the top-left corner; in landscape, it's on the left side of the screen about a third of the way down.)**

   To set this app to take videos, make sure that the video camera symbol is the larger of the two; if it isn't, tap the button again (refer to Figure 10-15).

4. **Tap the red Record button (see Figure 10-16).**

5. **When you're ready to stop recording video, tap the Stop button. (It replaced the Record button and looks like a small, white square in a red circle.)**

   Your video appears to the right of the Record button; tap it and tap again to play

Getting photos onto Kindle Fire HDX

When you first open the Photos app, you are offered a series of three screens that let you sync photos from your mobile phone, computer, and Facebook to your Kindle Fire with the touch of a button (see Figure 10-17).

If, at setup time, you didn't download some photos you need, you may want to get photos onto the device at a later time by saving an image from the Internet using your Silk browser, or by copying them from your computer using your micro USB cable (see the section "Getting Docs onto Kindle Fire HDX," at the start of this chapter, for more about this). Using this procedure, you can copy photos into the Pictures folder on your Kindle Fire HDX by using Windows Explorer or the Mac Finder.

Viewing photos

After you load photos into your Pictures library and disconnect the micro USB cable, you can tap the Photos app listed alongside other libraries on the Home screen. This app displays an album that represents the folder you copied to your Kindle Fire HDX (see Figure 10-18) and other albums for other sources, such as for downloads and screenshots. If you copy another folder of photos, it will come over as a separate album. Photos in albums are organized chronologically by the date you placed them on your Kindle Fire HDX.

Figure 10-16: Tap the big red button to begin recording.

There are three main actions you can perform to view pictures:

- ✔ Tap an album to open it and view the pictures within it.
- ✔ Tap a picture to make it appear full screen.
- ✔ Swipe left or right to move through pictures in an album.

You can also tap the E-mail button in the Share menu while in Photos to e-mail the displayed photo or post it to Facebook or Twitter. In the e-mail message that appears when you tap E-mail with the photo already attached, enter an address, subject, and a message (optional), and then tap the Send button.

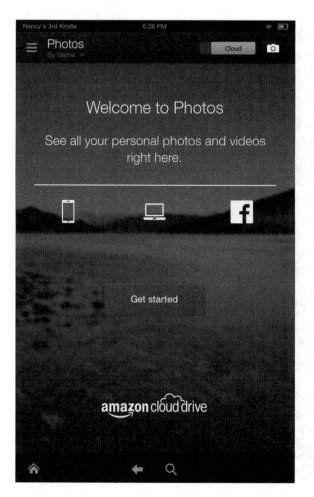

Figure 10-17: When you first open Photos, you are given an easy way to port content.

Editing photos

When you have captured a photo, you can use editing tools to modify it. The set of editing tools available in the latest edition of the Photos app are impressive: You can do everything from cropping and reducing red eye to rotating the photo, adjusting contrast and brightness, and even drawing or adding little stickers to a photo (this last is how I added a bow tie to my cat).

To edit a photo, follow these steps:

1. **On the Home screen, tap Photos in the libraries.**

2. **Locate a photo you want to edit and tap it.**

Figure 10-18: Photo albums in the Gallery.

3. **Tap the Menu button and then tap Edit.**

    In the screen that appears (see Figure 10-19), use the tools at the bottom of the screen to edit the photo. You can scroll to the right to see additional tools.

4. **To try some of these tools, tap the Rotate button and then tap the arrow buttons to rotate the image.**

5. **Tap the Back button on the Options bar to return to the main Edit screen.**

6. **Tap the Stickers button and choose an image such as eyeglasses or a heart to place on your photo; when the sticker appears, press on it and drag it to the place on the photo where you want it to appear.**

Figure 10-19: The Photos app offers 18 different editing tools.

7. Tap the Back button on the Options bar to return to the main Edit screen.

8. Tap the Crop button and then press and drag the corners of the crop area in or out to include the portion of the photo you want to keep; tap Apply to crop the image.

9. To save your edits, tap the Done button.

Editing tools are fun to explore; just open a photo and play around with all these amazing tools.

Managing photos in the Amazon Cloud Drive

Amazon Cloud Drive offers 5GB of free storage, which will accommodate about 2,000 photos. You can buy more storage by spending anywhere from $10 to $500 a year for it.

There are two things you can do to manage all those photos in the Cloud: Move photos from one album to another and rename photos or photo albums:

✔ **Moving photos:** To move a photo, you need to go to the Amazon Cloud Drive using a browser. (Go to Amazon.com, tap or click Your Account, and then tap or click Your Cloud Drive on the list that appears; you will have to sign in to your account at this point.) Select an album or photo and then use the More Actions drop-down list and choose Move *X* Items To. . . (where *X* is the number of items you've selected). Next, choose the folder on your Cloud Drive to move the item(s) to. If you choose Copy To instead of Move To, you create a copy in the destination folder.

✔ **Rename:** You can rename a picture or albums from within Cloud Drive by selecting an item, tapping or clicking the More Actions button, and then choosing Rename. You can also rename an album from your Kindle Fire HDX in the Photos app by long-pressing (pressing and holding for a few seconds) the album and choosing Rename from the menu that appears.

You can click the New Folder button to add albums to help you organize your photos. Then use the Moving photos directions described in the preceding list to move photos into the album.

Note that when viewing photos on your Kindle Fire HDX, you can also enlarge or reduce a photo by pinching and unpinching with your fingers on the touchscreen.

With a photo displayed, if you want to delete it, simply tap the Menu button and then tap Delete.

Using the Oxford Dictionary of English

If you tap the Books button and tap the On Device tab, you'll see the *Oxford Dictionary of English* in your book library. Amazon thoughtfully provided this book to help you find your way with words. (You may also find the slightly older *The New Oxford American Dictionary* on your Kindle Fire.)

In addition to being able to browse through the dictionary, when you press and hold a word in a book or magazine, a dictionary definition from the *Oxford Dictionary of English* is displayed (see Figure 10-20). You can tap the Full Definition button to go to the full dictionary entry.

When you open the dictionary, you can flick from page to page; entries are arranged here alphabetically, as with any dictionary.

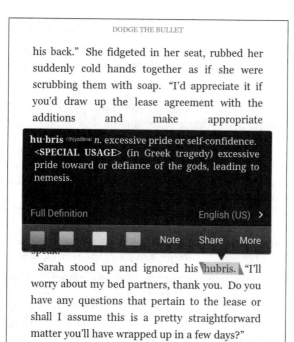

DODGE THE BULLET

his back." She fidgeted in her seat, rubbed her suddenly cold hands together as if she were scrubbing them with soap. "I'd appreciate it if you'd draw up the lease agreement with the additions and make appropriate

hu·bris /ˈ(h)yo͞obris/ *n.* excessive pride or self-confidence. <SPECIAL USAGE> (in Greek tragedy) excessive pride toward or defiance of the gods, leading to nemesis.

Full Definition   English (US) >

Note   Share   More

Sarah stood up and ignored his "hubris. "I'll worry about my bed partners, thank you. Do you have any questions that pertain to the lease or shall I assume this is a pretty straightforward matter you'll have wrapped up in a few days?"

"I can have it for you first thing tomorrow, *Mrs. Woodward*. Just don't say I didn't warn you."

She looked him in the eye and turned to leave without a proper goodbye. When she reached the sidewalk, she let out a shaky breath. She couldn't explain her anger, and didn't know who she was

2 hrs 57 mins left in book   36%

Figure 10-20: A definition displayed in an e-book.

As with any e-book, you can tap the View button at the top of the page to adjust font size, line spacing, margins, and the background color of the pages. You can also tap the Search button in the Options bar to locate a specific word. And you can tap the Left Nav button and sync to the last-read page (not so useful in a dictionary) or go to a specific page or location in the book (but this only uses a numerical location clear only to those at Amazon, so you might be better off dragging the progress bar to a later location or using the Search feature).

That's about all there is to the dictionary, but it can prove to be a handy resource for those who love words.

See Chapter 6 for more about reading all kinds of e-books on Kindle Fire HDX.

Part IV

The Part of Tens

Enjoy an additional Parts of Tens chapter online at www.dummies.com/extras/kindlefirehdx.

In this part...

- Explore ten apps that add great functionality to your Kindle Fire HDX.
- Have fun playing around with ten or so great gaming apps.

Ten Apps That Add Functionality to Kindle Fire HDX

In This Chapter

▸ Writing and drawing with your Kindle Fire HDX

▸ Going by the numbers

▸ Getting alarms

▸ Monitoring your connection

*A*ny mobile device today, from a smartphone to a tablet, depends on the thousands of apps that make a world of features available.

Kindle Fire HDX has functionality built in for consuming books, periodicals, music, and video, as well as a contact management and calendar app, web browser, and e-mail client. However, there are some tools that many of us have grown used to having available that you can easily acquire by adding apps to the device.

Amazon Appstore, which you learn the ins and outs of using in Chapter 4, contains thousands of cool apps for you to explore. To help you flesh out the basic tools in Kindle Fire HDX, in this chapter, I provide reviews of apps such as a note taker and unit converter that meet your day-to-day needs and whet your appetite. Most of these are free.

From a nutrition guide to a very cool drawing app, these apps will provide you fun and useful functionality for your Kindle Fire HDX and not cost you much more than the time to download them.

SketchBook Mobile

From: AutoDesk, Inc.

Price: $1.99

SketchBook (see Figure 11-1) is a drawing app to satisfy the creative artist in your soul. With 47 preset brushes, you can draw whatever you can imagine on your Kindle Fire HDX screen. You can control the brush characteristics and make use of an extensive color palette.

Try sideloading photos and modifying them with this clever app, then save your files in JPEG, PNG, or PSD formats. When you are done, it's easy to e-mail your artistic efforts to yourself to print from your computer.

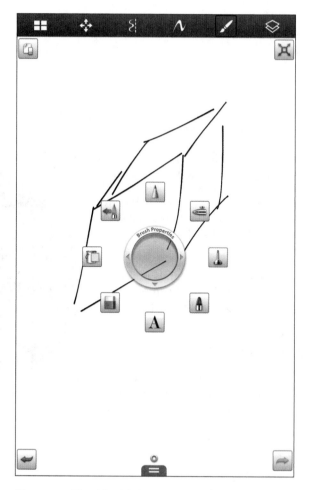

Figure 11-1: Sketchbook brings out the artist in you.

The Brush Properties circular control lets you easily adjust the size and opacity of the writing tools. Touch the square at the top of the screen to access color controls and watch the Red, Blue, and Green levels adjust as you move around the color wheel.

However, be careful of the Erase button in the upper-left corner of the screen: I've erased more than one picture by tapping this when I shouldn't have!

Calorie Counter and Diet Tracker

From: MyFitnessPal, LLC

Price: Free

If you need a bit of help in keeping those pounds off, a calorie counter could come in handy. MyFitness Pal (see Figure 11-2) is a simple-to-use app with a pretty huge food database containing more than 3 million food listings. You can also enter your exercise information to help you balance your intake with your burn.

NUTRIENT DETAILS	Total	Goal	Left
Total Fat (g)	0	72	72
Saturated (g)	0	24	24
Polyunsaturated (g)	0	N/A	N/A
Monounsaturated (g)	0	N/A	N/A
Trans (g)	0	0	0
Cholesterol (mg)	0	300	300
Sodium (mg)	0	2500	2500
Potassium (mg)	0	3500	3500
Total Carbs (g)	0	296	296
Dietary Fiber (g)	0	25	25
Sugars (g)	0	43	43
Protein (g)	0	81	81
Vitamin A	0%	100%	100%
Vitamin C	0%	100%	100%
Calcium	0%	100%	100%
Iron	0%	100%	100%

SATURDAY | OCT 19, 2013

Figure 11-2: Keep track of your calories with this handy counter.

A handy feature is the ability to scan barcodes to enter foods quickly. You can save the calories from an entire meal and create custom foods if you are your favorite creative chef. You can even create custom exercises (shark wrestling anyone?).

To keep you motivated, you can set personal goals and even get progress reports. If you are a real nutrition control freak, you'll be happy to see that this app helps you keep track of calories, fat, protein, carbohydrates, sugar, fiber, and cholesterol.

Alarm Clock Xtreme Free

From: AVG Technologies

Price: Free

Kindle Fire HDX Calendar allows you set reminders that appear in Notifications, but if you require an alarm clock to rouse you to action, this one is a natural to add to your apps collection. This easy-to-use alarm app can help keep you on schedule (see Figure 11-3). You can create and edit alarms and control how far ahead of events and at what intervals you're alerted to alarms.

Figure 11-3: Get alarms to get you going on time.

You can set a timer with this app and have the app display a countdown to the event (countdown to Christmas, countdown to your wedding day, countdown till your soufflé is done; your choice!). You can change the look and feel of the alarm app with different colored backgrounds and a large Snooze button.

Astral Budget

From: Astral Web, Inc.

Price: Free

If you're like many of us, these days, you are tightening your belt and counting those pennies. Astral Budget is an app that helps you keep track of all your expenses, whether for a single trip or your yearly household budget. You can use built-in categories for fixed spending such as rent, food, travel, utilities, and so on to categorize your expenses.

The app has four sections: Goals, Expense, Reports, and Export (see Figure 11-4). Using these, you can enter the amounts you want to spend and track them against actual expenditures. You can use the wide variety of Reports in Astral Budget to examine your spending trends and even export data to your computer to examine with the more-robust application Excel. I like the Chart selections, including bar charts, pie charts, and list charts.

Figure 11-4: Use various tools to enter and visualize your spending practices.

ColorNote Notepad Notes

From: Social & Mobile, Inc.

Price: Free

Kindle Fire HDX has OfficeSuite Pro available on Amazon Cloud with free downloading for word processing, but it doesn't include a note-taking app, and if you're like me, you need one. If being able to keep a to-do list warms the cockles of your organized (or disorganized) heart, this is a neat little free app, and it's very simple to use.

You can keep a simple to-do list or other random notes, and even share information with your friends via e-mail, social networks, or messaging (honey, here's the shopping list for your evening commute!).

ColorNote allows some nice word-processing-like functions, such as the ability to edit and delete completed items from lists (see Figure 11-5).

You can even set up reminders for items in your notes and search for specific content.

If your notes are top secret, consider using the password feature in ColorNote.

Calculator Plus Free

From: Digitalchemy, LLC

Price: Free

It's a good idea to add a calculator to Kindle Fire HDX, if only to figure out tips at restaurants and your sales commissions, right?

Calculator Plus Free works great on Kindle Fire HDX. You can see where you are in your calculation so that you don't lose track when entering a long list of numbers. The design and typeface used in the app are attractive and easy to read (see Figure 11-6).

If you make a mistake, no worries: Tap Backspace and you can correct your mistake then and there. The memory feature can store a running total as you work. If you want more advanced math features, you just swipe the memory keys, and they appear.

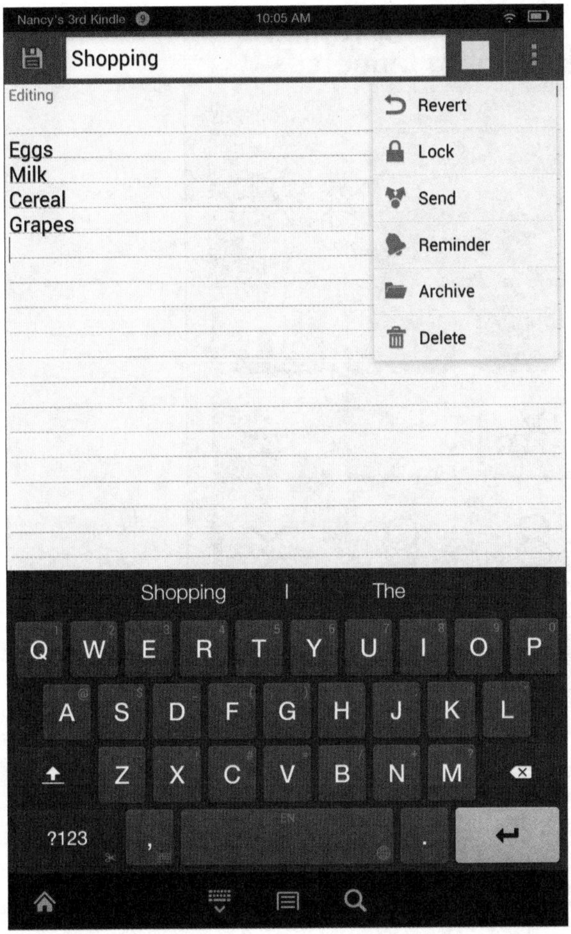

Figure 11-5: When you finish an item on your list, delete it.

AccuWeather

From: AccuWeather

Price: Free

Many people use AccuWeather every day from their smartphone or computer to get a glimpse of what to expect today or tomorrow, whether that be sunny skies or a blizzard.

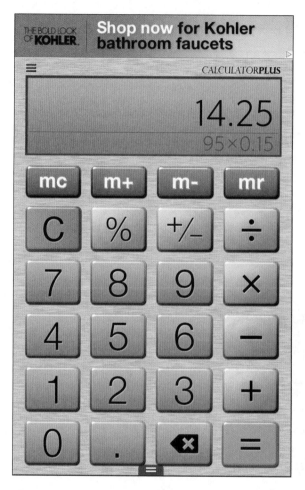

Figure 11-6: The interface of Calculator Plus Free is well designed.

AccuWeather is available for Kindle Fire, and it offers weather forecasts for more than 2.7 million places in the world in 27 languages. Forecasts are updated every 15 minutes so that you can stay current on weather conditions (see Figure 11-7).

You can get longer-range forecasts for up to 15 days from today to help you plan trips or other events. Of course, don't forget that the further out the forecast, the more chances that things will change by the time that day rolls around.

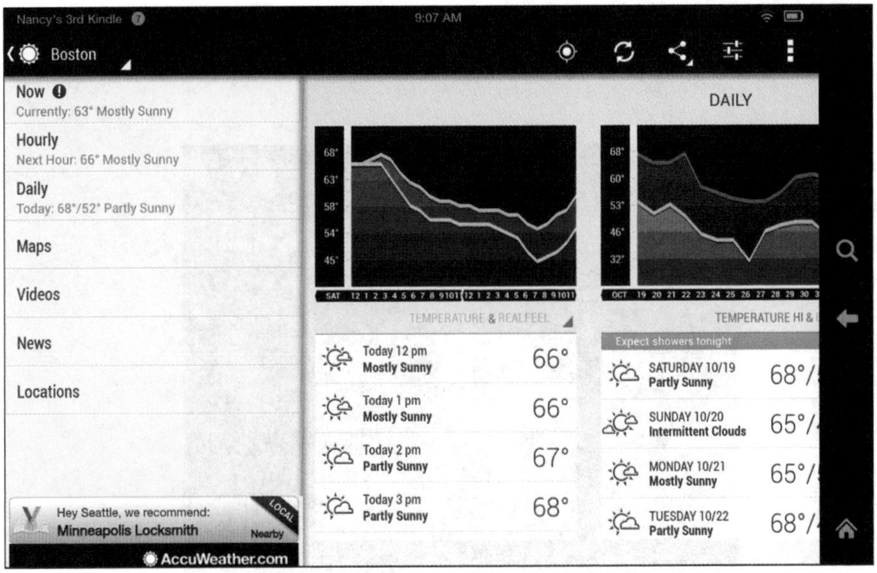

Figure 11-7: AccuWeather could keep you warmer and drier with its weather predictions.

AccuWeather works using radar and satellites along with Google Maps to give you a picture of weather such as oncoming rain fronts. Weather graphs help you spot weather trends.

You can set up custom forecasts; for example, if you have asthma and need to know about weather conditions that could affect your respiration or you are a runner who needs alerts for when weather will make running conditions poor.

Bloomberg (Kindle Tablet Edition)

From: Bloomberg L.P.

Price: Free

If investing is your thing, you'll find this stock reporting and tracking tool incredibly useful. The information is up to the minute and features both stock quotes and financial news. You can find updates on equity, commodity, bond, and currency market activity, as well as industry data and stock prices.

You can create a portfolio of your investments to help you track them more easily, and even watch videos about top financial news stories right on your Kindle Fire HDX.

All in all you can get a very comprehensive picture of what is driving current financial conditions all from within this one app (see Figure 11-8). Check out the Exclusive list to read stories from Bloomberg's own insightful editors.

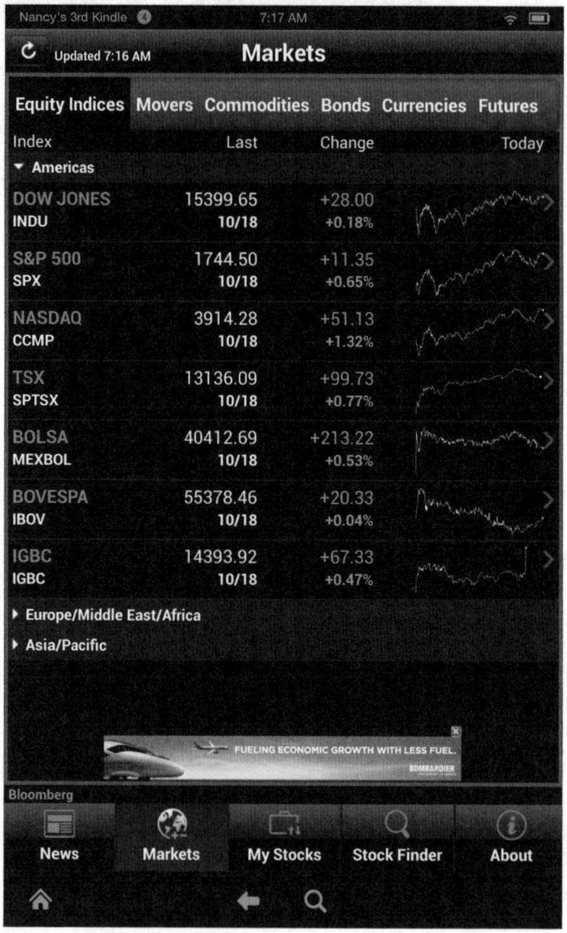

Figure 11-8: Get a good feel for finances with Bloomberg.

Convertr

From: Vervv LLC

Price: $1.99

If, like me, you need help converting just about anything to anything else (feet to meters, pounds to kilos, or whatever), you'll appreciate this handy little app with a clean, uncluttered interface (see Figure 11-9). Here are the things you can convert using this app:

- Angle
- Area
- Currency
- Data Rate
- Data Size
- Density
- Energy
- Force
- Frequency (disabled by default)
- Fuel
- Length
- Mass and Weight
- Power
- Pressure
- Speed
- Temperature
- Time
- Torque
- Typography
- Volume

If you're scientifically minded, you'll be glad to know that you can get your conversion to up to 12 decimal points. Each conversion category has multiple options; for example, the Length category has 26 conversion units and Volume has 48. Currency alone has 67 different options, and Convertr updates currency prices constantly.

Figure 11-9: Convert temperature scales easily.

Wifi Analyzer

From: farproc

Price: Free

Because Kindle Fire HDX can connect to the web only through Wi-Fi, with the exception of the model that can use 4G LTE to connect, this handy app is helpful for keeping track of local Wi-Fi connections. You can observe available Wi-Fi channels and the signal strength on each (see Figure 11-10). There are several styles of graph to choose from, including Channel, Time, Channel Rating, and Signal Meter.

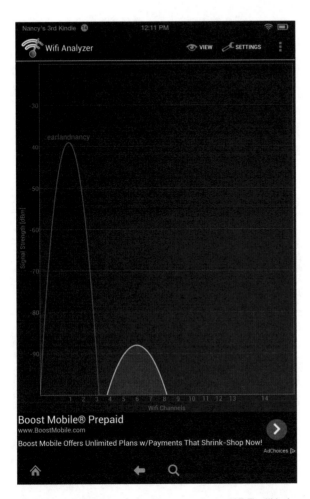

Figure 11-10: Figure out whether your nearest Wi-Fi will help you connect.

Ten (or So) Top Gaming Apps

In This Chapter

▶ Testing your reflexes

▶ Puzzling with words

▶ Playing the classics

*P*eople using tablets will tell you that one great way to use them is to play games of all sorts. From card games such as solitaire to graphically entertaining new classics like Contre Jour and Where's My Perry?, having access to games helps you while away a quiet evening at home or keep yourself from getting bored in boring settings, such as the security line at the airport or the dentist's waiting room.

With Kindle Fire HDX, you get an accelerometer, gyroscope, and Adreno 330 GPU, technobabble for features that let your games live large. Think tilting your HDX to move around the streets of Tokyo in a race car or shaking up your onscreen world in a battle between titans. Trust me, it's cool.

Be sure to check out GameCircle, Amazon's new combination of social networking and gaming. Open the Games library and tap Connect to connect through Facebook and find friends who are using Amazon GameCircle. You can then share scores, achievements, and the games that you love to play with others.

In this chapter, I introduce you to 12 great games that will provide hours of fun and create the core of your Kindle Fire gaming library.

Contre Jour

From: Chillingo

Price: $1.99

This game has been called the intellectual's Cut the Rope because it uses the same premise of swinging a creature around a space to land on the winning spot, but in a much more sophisticated environment (see Figure 12-1). Against its black-and-white abstract art background that would warm Salvador Dali's heart, you're challenged to move a little one-eyed blob around to collect bits of light.

The game involves prodding the landscape to reshape it and thereby roll or push the creature toward the lights. There are also tentacles that you can use to latch on to the creature and swing it toward the lights.

To complete the game, your little blob must hit the big ball of light. Remember to collect other bits of light along the way to rack up higher scores. A lovely little piece of music plays in the background, but you can turn it off when you inevitably get tired of it. This is a fun, mentally challenging, one-person game worth checking out.

Figure 12-1: Use what's at hand to send your blob into the light.

Monsters Ate My Condo

From: Adult Swim Games

Price: $0.99

This colorful and peppy game has you tossing colored boxes (condos) in monsters' mouths (see Figure 12-2). The point of the game is to move the boxes so that three or more of one color are placed together in the stack of boxes. When this happens, those boxes disappear and the stack is straightened up again. You can achieve this goal by tossing boxes of different colors into either of the two monsters. As you toss things, you have to be sure the stack of boxes doesn't topple; if it does, you lost.

Figure 12-2: Use condo power to keep the monsters happy and keep your stack from toppling.

There are lots of rules about what actions will make the monsters angry, such as feeding them condos of a color that's different from their color. Also, concrete blocks sometimes appear in the stack, and you have to do some fancy maneuvering around them because they can't be moved.

My advice is to turn off the annoying music and just have fun flinging boxes — and don't even wonder why monsters would want to eat condos. If you do get a high score, prepare for a large, animated woman to sing her praises in an operatic voice.

Where's My Perry?

From: Disney

Price: $0.99

Based on the cartoon character Perry the Platypus, otherwise known as Agent P, this game is probably my favorite of the bunch. Perry is trapped underground in a little glass cage, and you have to set him free (see Figure 12-3). To do that, you release water, steam, or ice into the pipe leading to his chamber. Using these materials, you can dig tunnels in the earth.

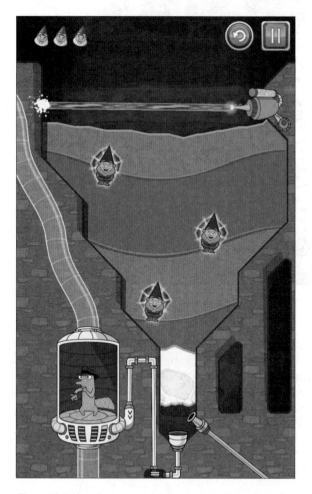

Figure 12-3: Help Perry escape his cage with the power of water.

However, along the way you'll encounter lots of interesting variations. Sometimes you release steam to trigger a mechanism that opens a gate and allows water to come through. Sometimes you have to figure out how to melt ice into water with a laser. Don't forget to whack as many gnomes as you can along the way to score more points.

Figuring out how to free Perry each time takes real problem-solving skills and makes for a game that challenges your brain. Despite the Disney connection, this one is great for kids and adults.

Quell Memento

From: Fallen Tree Games

Price: $2.99

Quell is a peaceful afternoon in the park compared to some of the other games listed here. It doesn't involve monsters or sword fights. Instead, you get a playing board with a small raindrop on it. You can move the raindrop up or down a row to collect the pearly objects in its path while peaceful oriental music plays in the background.

The trick is that you have to figure out how to get the raindrop to hit objects not already in its path. Sometimes, you have to shift the raindrop from one side of the board to the other, move up, then over, then down, and so on until you're in line with the object you want to hit (see Figure 12-4).

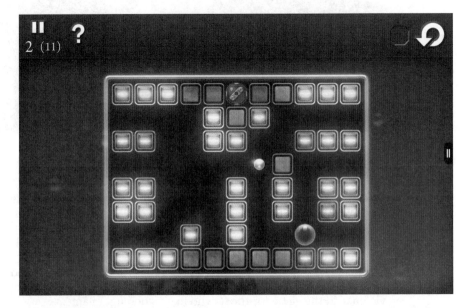

Figure 12-4: This little brain teaser will keep your mind sharp.

As you proceed through levels, you get new challenges that require some brain power. But the whole experience is much more relaxing and peaceful than many games you find these days.

Blood and Glory: Legend

From: Glu Mobile

Price: Free

If you're into the bloody battle kind of game, which I'm not, you'll find the graphics on this gladiator game to be very high end. With you as the gladiator, you get to slash your sword and heft your shield against a variety of monstrous opponents, as shown in Figure 12-5.

Figure 12-5: Fight the good fight for your emperor in this slash — up game.

You tap a button to raise your shield in defense, and swipe across the screen to lunge with your sword. The game definitely challenges your reflexes as you try to stay alive in the battle. As you play, you can buy new skills to help you succeed; you pay real money to obtain these skills in the form of digital content.

The quality animations and back story about the heroic gladiator trying to defend the emperor from mutant attackers may be enough to justify the violence in the game for those who like a good fight game.

Stray Souls: Dollhouse Story

From: Alawar Entertainment

Price: $2.99

This is your typical, creepy-old-house, found-objects game, and it's a very well-executed one at that. Two newlyweds are at home one evening when a knock comes on the door. A package has been left on the doorstep, and the husband instantly disappears. The game involves the wife looking for clues to where he might have gone.

As you move around to different locations (like the one shown in Figure 12-6), looking for clues, you have to pick up items such as pliers to open the package and a key to unlock a drawer. You pick up items like a torn photo and have to search for the other half. The music is appropriately creepy, and the "plot" is clever.

Figure 12-6: Solve the mystery by accumulating objects.

You can get hints if you are stuck, and there's a strategy guide for each chapter of play. You can also choose your level of play: casual or expert.

Chess Free

From: Optime Software

Price: Free

If chess is your thing, you'll enjoy this electronic version. You can play the computer or play against another person using the same Kindle Fire. With the latter approach, the board swaps around after each play so that the next person can take his or her turn. There's a game timer if you're in Chess Tournament mode. You can also change the style of the pieces and board.

Tap a piece, and then the game shows you all possible moves unless you turn off Show Legal and Last Moves in the game's Options. Tap the place on the board where you want to move the piece (see Figure 12-7). In case you have a change of heart, this game includes a handy Undo button.

Figure 12-7: If you love chess, try this version.

Bejeweled 2

From: PopCap Games

Price: $2.99

If you have a thing about jewelry, or even if you don't, you might enjoy this matching game that lets you play with jewel-colored baubles to your heart's content. The idea is that you can flip two gems on this grid-like game board if doing so will allow you to line up three items of the same kind (see Figure 12-8). When you do, the lines of gems shift to provide a different arrangement.

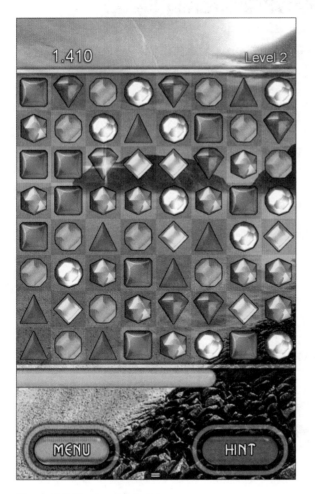

Figure 12-8: Simple yet colorful.

The game has a few other rules, such as getting more points for chain reactions and scoring bonus points. The game is over when no more possible three-of-a-kind matches are left.

Wordsmith

From: Second Breakfast Studios

Price: $2.49

Wordsmith is kind of like the popular word game Scrabble. You build words from available tiles and take advantage of double-letter and triple-word tiles (as shown in Figure 12-9) to score extra points.

Figure 12-9: Scrabble fan alert! Wordsmith gets your spelling mojo on.

The game definitely gets you thinking about how to utilize tiles already in place to one-up yourself or your opponent. The game accommodates two to four players. Build your vocabulary while having fun with Wordsmith.

As with many games, this one comes in a free version, as well. Free versions may include advertisements and offer more limited levels of play.

Solitaire Free Pack

From: Tesseract Mobile Software

Price: Free

This game doesn't have too many surprises, but for those who are devoted to solitaire, it offers an electronic version that you can play on the go on your Kindle Fire HDX (see Figure 12-10). Rack up the points with 50 different games, including Klondike, Pyramid, and Monte Carlo.

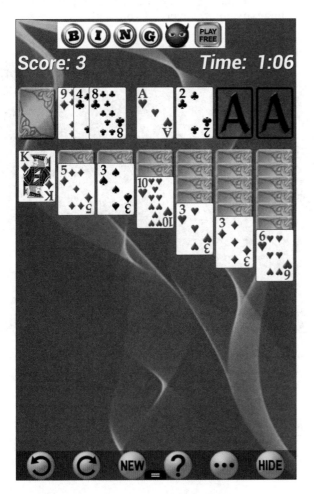

Figure 12-10: If you're alone, try a round of solitaire.

You can change the card backgrounds and track your game scores to see whether you're improving as you go. If you want, you can take advantage of the unlimited redo feature to try and try again to win a game.

Asphalt 8: Airborne

From: Gameloft

Price: $0.99

If you love to race fast cars, this game will give you that experience on your Kindle Fire HDX with sharp graphics and quick moves. You can play around with more than 150 races with any of several vehicles in a wide variety of settings (see Figure 12-11). You can play locally on your Kindle Fire HDXor with up to six people online in a multiplayer environment.

Figure 12-11: Do you fancy a DeLorean, a Ferrari, or a Lamborghini? They're all available here to test drive on tracks from Paris to Hawaii.

Beware: This game has drop-dead gorgeous graphics, but the trade off is that you'll eat up a big chunk of your device's storage when you download it.

Words with Friends Free

From: Zynga Game Network

Price: Free

The appeal of this game is that you can play it with others. Available for both iPad/iPhone and Android devices, like your Kindle Fire HDX, the game involves building words, à la Scrabble (see Figure 12-12). However, you can also send back and forth chat bubbles as you play.

Figure 12-12: Connect with friends to build words and score points.

And one for the traditional gamers

When I'm feeling like having a mellow gaming experience, I like Random Mahjong (Paul Burkey, Free) because there are no time limits and no super bonus points to earn. You just take your time matching the nicely designed tiles layer by layer. You can control the look of the game and get hints when your brain is getting tired. This is a good way to relax between rounds of Fruit Ninja and Jetpack Joyride. Search the Games store for other old friends in the world of games; you might be surprised at what you'll find!

You and your friend take turns building words either horizontally or vertically on the board. The game is over when one of you has used up all your tiles. Along the way there are double and triple scoring options. The list of acceptable words is based on the Enhanced North American Benchmark Lexicon, which is a common set of words used in many games; however, this game's authors have added a few more contemporary words for online gamers, such as *texting*.

Index

• *Numerics* •

1-Tap-Archive, 8
4g LTE considerations, 11

• *A* •

Accessibility Tools
  closed captioning, 73
  Large Fonts, toggling, 73
  overview, 8
  Screen Magnifier, 73
  Screen Reader, 71
  shortcut gestures, 72
  stereo/mono conversion, 73
  User's Guides, 73
AccuWeather app, 231–233
ADB (app debugging), 63
Airplane Mode
  Settings, accessing from, 66
  toggling on/off, 52
Alarm Clock Xtreme Free app, 228
Amazon
  account creation, 77
  account registering/deregistering,
    55–56, 78–98
  account settings, managing, 79
  Amazon Coins, 83–84
  Appstore, accessing, 80
  audio book availability, 15
  Bookstore, accessing, 91
  content availability, 15–17
  downloading automatically, 126
  Kindle Fire registrations, 31, 78–79
  Lending Library, 17, 126
  Music Importer, installing/using, 156
  Newsstand, buying magazines, 87–90
  Shop Amazon app, 97–98
  Video store, accessing/shopping, 95–97

Amazon Assist (Mayday)
  Help button, accessing with, 57
  overview, 53–54
Amazon Cloud Drive
  computer, transferring content from, 48
  managing device storage with, 10–11, 36
  moving content to, 37–38
  music, accessing from, 94, 157
  Newsstand, downloading with, 89–90
  photos, managing, 221
  retrieving content from, 37
  sideloaded docs, 200
  storage limitations, 12–13
  syncing computer to Kindle, 200–201
  uploading music to, 155–157
Amazon Coins, 83
Amazon Prime
  membership advantages, 19–21, 128
  streaming video access, 20
Amazon Videos store
  accessing/opening, 170
  navigating categories, 170–171
  Videos button, accessing with, 167–168
app debugging (ADB), 63
apps (applications). *See also*
Appstore
  AccuWeathe, 231–233
  Alarm Clock Xtreme Free, 228
  android app issues, 80
  Asphalt 8: Airborne, 250
  Astral Budget, 228–229
  Bejeweled 2, 247
  Blood and Glory: Legend, 244
  Bloomberg (Kindle Tablet Edition),
    233–234
  Calculator Plus Free app, 230–232
  Calorie Counter and Diet Tracker, 227
  Chess Free, 246
  ColorNote Notepad Notes, 230–231

Appstore *(continued)*
  Contre Jour app, 239–240
  Convertr app, 235
  deleting, 86
  downloading, 14–15, 84–86
  downloading requirements, 14
  Force Stop button, using, 68
  FreeTime, 8, 39, 58
  gaming, overview, 239
  Kindle reading, 128
  Mahjong, 252
  managing, 67–68
  Newsstand, 16, 45–46, 87–90, 126,
      147–148
  Monsters Ate my Condo,
      240–241
  notifications management, 69
  overview, 80
  parental controls, setting, 59
  pre-installed, 12, 181
  purchasing, 84
  Quell Memento, 243–244
  reading (computer), 128
  sideloading, 13
  SketchBook Mobile, 226–227
  Solitaire Free Pack, 249–250
  Stray Souls: Dollhouse Story, 245
  Today's Free App of the Day, 80
  Where's My Perry? 242–243
  Wifi Analyzer, 236–237
  Words with Friends Free, 251
  Wordsmith, 248–249
Apps button
  Amazon Appstore, 16, 80
  Home screen location, 12
  social networks, using with, 33
Appstore. *See also* apps
  accessing from Kindle, 80
  app descriptions, accessing, 82
  navigating with swipes, 80
  periodicals, browsing/purchasing,
      87–90
  purchases, completing, 84–86
  searching versus browsing, 80–83
  Today's Free App of the Day, 80
Asphalt 8: Airborne app, 250
Astral Budget app, 228–229

Audible
  audiobook availability, 15
  downloading, 136
  Immersion Reading, using for,
      135–136
audiobooks
  Immersion Reading, 135–136
  playing from Books library, 136
  pre-installed functionality, 12
  Whispersync, syncing with, 126
Auto Correction settings, 71
Auto-Capitalization settings, 71
Auto-Rotate, 50–51

• *B* •

battery
  charging, 31–32
  power saving (sleep), 70
Bejeweled 2 app, 247
Blood and Glory: Legend app, 244
Bloomberg (Kindle Tablet Edition) app,
      233–234
Bluetooth settings, 67
bookmarks, 103, 106
books
  bookmarking pages, 141
  Bookstore, accessing, 126
  brightness settings, 51, 70–71, 145
  definitions, finding, 221
  dictionary definitions, accessing, 143
  fixed layout constraints, 135
  Grid View versus List View, 130–131
  highlighting text, 141–142
  Kindle device library, opening, 130
  lending library, using, 127–128
  loaning to others, 129
  locating/opening, 132–133
  navigating, 132–133
  new download identification, 131
  option bar, displaying, 133
  page appearance, modifying,
      143–146
  progress bar, 135
  Search the Web option, 140
  searching within, 138–139

social networks, sharing through, 146, 189–191
sorting options, 131–132
viewing tools, displaying, 133–134
X-Ray feature, using, 137–138
Books library
active tab, identifying, 130
Grid View/List View toggle, 130–131
opening books, 132–133
sorting options, 131–132
Bookstore
downloading options, 126
e-books, downloading from, 91–92
Brightness settings
Display & Sounds settings, 70–71
manual/automatic adjustments, 145
Quick Settings, using, 51
browser
bookmarks, managing, 103, 106
browsing history, clearing, 114
browsing history, using, 111–112
Cloud-accelerated advantages, 17, 101
downloading content, 113
form data, remembering/clearing, 115
Home screen, accessing from, 101
Internet searching, 109–111
libraries, opening from, 35
location services, enabling/clearing, 115
navigation aids, 101
overview, 101
photos, downloading, 216
photos, viewing/saving options, 113
predictive pre-loading, 17
privacy issues, 18, 107
privacy settings, 114–116
Reading View, using, 103–104
search engines, choosing, 110–111
searching pages, 108–109
settings, clearing, 116
settings, overview, 106–108
shortcuts panel, 104–105
tabs, managing, 102
website data, clearing, 116
budget app, 228–229

● C ●

cache
clearing, 114, 155
definition, 101
Silk browser, speeding access, 101
Calculator Plus Free app, 230–232
Calendar app
events, adding, 213
navigating, 212
repeat events, scheduling, 213
syncing through e-mail, 211–213
Calorie Counter and Diet Tracker app, 227
Camera app
still pictures, taking, 214–215
video recording, 216
Carousel
content, opening, 38
Favorites area, adding items to, 40
overview, 33–34
charging, 31–32
Chess Free app, 246
Clips feature, 202
closed captioning, 73
Cloud Collection feature, 152
Cloud Drive
computer, transferring content from, 48
computer installation, 48
managing device storage with, 10–11, 36
moving content to, 37–38
music, accessing from, 94, 157
music, uploading to, 155–157
Newsstand, downloading with, 89–90
photos, managing, 221
retrieving content from, 37
sideloaded docs, 200
storage limitations, 12–13
syncing computer to Kindle, 200–201
Cloud Drive Installer, 48
Coins, 83
ColorNote Notepad Notes app, 230
Contacts app
contacts, viewing/organizing, 187–188
importing contacts, 182–183
locating, 181

Contacts app *(continued)*
  new accounts, adding, 183
  new contacts, creating, 183–185
  opening in Favorites, 188
  photo, adding, 185–186
  Skype, using with, 193
content
  availability, 15–17
  Carousel, viewing from, 38–39
  Cloud versus device storage, 36
  downloading, 113
  libraries, accessing through, 34–38
  Newsstand, managing, 148
  parental controls, setting, 17, 58–60
  Quickswitch, accessing with, 38
  sharing to Facebook, 189–191
  Silk filtering/prediction, 17
  transferring from computer to Amazon
    Cloud Drive, 48
  video storage recommendations, 38
Contre Jour app, 239–240
Convertr app, 235
cookies, managing, 114
credential storage, 73–74
Customer Service, accessing, 57

• D •

Date & Time settings, 62–63
device administrators, 73–74
device libraries. *See also* libraries
  Apps library, managing, 80, 85–86
  audiobooks, playing, 136
  book samples, deleting, 148
  Books library, opening, 130, 132
  display options, 130–132
  displaying, 147
  Docs library, 113, 122
  downloading versus streaming, 148
  Music, 16, 35–38, 94–95, 152–153
  Newsstand, 45, 87–90
  removing items, 91, 148
  restoring books from Cloud, 147–148
  Videos, 35, 97
Device settings
  Accessibility Tools, 71–73
  app debugging, 63

application management, 67–68
battery information, 61–62
Date & Time, 62–63
Display & Sounds, 69–71
language choices, 62
Notifications management, 69
onscreen keyboard settings, 71
power saving (sleep), 70
Reset to Factory Defaults, 64–65
serial number display, 64
storage information, 63
system updates, 62
Text-to-Speech choices, 62
Wireless options, 66–67
dictionaries
  adding/managing, 71
  Oxford Dictionary of English, 221–222
dieting app, 227
display
  mirroring, 70
  sleep adjustments, 70–71
Display & Sounds settings
  sleep function, 70–71
  TV/monitor mirroring, 70
  volume control, 69
Docs library
  Clips feature, 202
  folders, creating, 204
  opening, 198
  documents, opening, 203–205
  documents, searching for, 205
  documents, sideloading, 199–200
  documents, sorting, 204
documents
  Docs library, opening, 198
  editing in OfficeSuite, 209–211
  e-mail to Kindle, 200
  e-mailing as attachments, 205–207
  formats supported, 202–203
  graphic files supported, 203
  OfficeSuite pre-installed, 12, 197
  opening from Docs library, 203–204
  opening in OfficeSuite, 209
  pre-installed reader functionality, 12
  printing options, 207–208
  searching for, 205
  sideloading to Docs library, 199–200

syncing through Cloud Drive, 200–201
transferring/reading, 149–150
Zip files, 203
Dolby Digital Plus, 151
downloading
    Amazon, 126
    apps, 14–15, 84–86
    content from Internet browser, 113
    e-books with Bookstore app, 91–92
    images, 216
    with Newsstand app, 87–90
    storage options, 36
    streaming versus, 35, 167–168
    Whispersync, using for, 14, 36
drawing app, 226–227
Dropbox, 209

• E •

e-books
    Amazon Bookstore, accessing, 91
    bookmarking pages, 141
    Bookstore, downloading with, 91–92
    brightness settings, 51, 70–71, 145
    browsing for, 91
    definitions, finding, 221
    deleting, 91
    dictionary definitions, accessing, 143
    fixed layout constraints, 135
    highlighting text, 141–142
    Left Nav button, using, 134
    library borrowing, 90
    navigating, 133–134
    option bar, displaying, 133
    page appearance, modifying, 143–146
    page turning, 133
    progress bar, 135
    Search the Web option, 140
    searching within, 138–139
    social networks, sharing through, 146,
        189–191
    Text-to-Speech, using with, 145
    viewing tools, displaying, 133–134
    X-Ray feature, using, 137–138
e-mail
    attachments, 205–207
    Calendar app, syncing, 211–213

carousel, accessing from, 26
contact records, adding pictures, 185–186
creating/sending, 117
documents, attaching, 205–207
documents, to Kindle, 200
forwarding, 120
Kindle account, finding, 200
Kindle account, using, 121–122
Kindle Fire account, 31
marking as read/unread, 121
notifications, 27, 42
overview, 116
photo sharing options, 48, 117, 217
pictures, receiving, 31
receiving/saving/deleting, 118
replying, options for, 119–121
set-up screen, 116–117
text shortcuts, 117
e-reader (app)
    bookmarking pages, 141
    brightness settings, 51, 70–71, 145
    dictionary definitions, accessing, 143
    fixed layout constraints, 135
    highlighting text, 141–142
    Home screen, returning to, 129
    Left Nav button, 134
    navigating, 133–134
    option bar, displaying, 133
    overview, 125
    page appearance, modifying, 143–146
    page turning, 133
    pre-installed functionality, 12
    progress bar, 135
    Search the Web option, 140
    searching within books, 138–139
    social networks, sharing through, 146
    viewing tools, displaying, 133–134
    X-Ray feature, 137–138

• F •

Facebook
    accounts, setting up, 30
    app download, 189
    photo sharing options, 48
    pre-installed functionality, 12
    sharing content from Kindle, 189–191

factory defaults, resetting, 64–66
Favorites area
    Contacts app, 188
    default apps, 39–40
    overview, 38
    pinning new items, 40
    removing items, 40–41
Feedback feature, accessing, 57–58, 60
file formats, 202–203
files
    e-mail attachments, 205–207
    pre-installed, 65
    sideloading, 46–47, 199–200, 216, 226
    streaming versus downloading, 168
    syncing with Cloud, 200–201, 211–213
financial investment app, 233–234
fixed layout constraints, 135
flinging movies, 13, 177
fonts
    book settings, 133
    e-books, enlarging/reducing, 143–144, 222
    fixed layout constraints, 135
    large size, toggling, 73
    OfficeSuite, changing in, 210
Force Stop button, 68
4g LTE considerations, 11
FreeTime app
    Favorites area, accessing from, 39
    overview, 8
    Parental Controls, settings in, 58

• G •

GameCircle, 239
gaming apps
    Asphalt 8: Airborne, 250
    Bejeweled 2, 247
    Blood and Glory: Legend, 244
    Chess Free, 246
    Contre Jour, 239–240
    Mahjong, 252
    Monsters Ate my Condo, 240–241
    overview, 239
    Quell Memento, 243–244
    Solitaire Free Pack, 249–250
    Stray Souls: Dollhouse Story, 245
    Where's My Perry? 242–243
    Words with Friends Free, 251
    Wordsmith, 248–249
gestures. *See also* swipe gestures
    double-tapping, 28, 72, 117, 135,
        148–149
    photos, enlarging/reducing, 221
    pinching/unpinching, 28, 73, 149
Goodreads
    overview, 8
    virtual book club, 126
graphics (photos)
    album organization, 216, 221
    Cloud Drive, managing in, 221
    Contacts app, adding to,
        185–186
    deleting, 221
    downloading methods, 216
    editing options, 218–220
    email, receiving pictures, 31
    file formats supported, 203
    sharing methods, 48, 217
    social networks, sharing through,
        189–191
    taking with Camera app, 214–215
    viewing options, 217
    viewing/editing, 12
    viewing/saving options, 113–114
Grid View
    Books library, toggling in, 130–131
    e-mail access, 116
    overview, 8
    Silk browser access, 101

• H •

hardware specifications, 9–10
Help button (Settings), 57–58
history (browser)
    clearing, 114
    using, 111–112
Home button
    Options bar, using from, 45
    overview, 28

Home screen
  Apps button, 12, 80
  Books, 91–92
  bypassing with gestures, 8
  Carousel, using, 38
  Favorites thumbnails, 38–40
  Grid view, 8
  Home button, returning with, 28, 46
  libraries, accessing, 16
  Music, 92–95
  Newsstand, 88–90
  overview, 26
  photos, sharing from, 48
  Quick Settings, displaying, 27, 99
  Quickswitch, accessing, 38
  Silk browser, accessing, 101
  Status bar indicators, 32
  unlock button, opening with, 28
  Videos, 95–97

● **I** ●

icons used in book, 2
images
  album organization, 216, 221
  Cloud Drive, managing in, 221
  Contacts app, adding to, 185–186
  deleting, 221
  downloading methods, 216
  editing options, 218–220
  email, receiving pictures, 31
  file formats supported, 203
  sharing methods, 48, 217
  social networks, sharing through,
      189–191
  taking with Camera app,
      214–215
  viewing options, 217
  viewing/editing, 12
  viewing/saving options, 113–114
Immersion Reading
  Audible app, using for, 136
  definition, 15
  locating/purchasing, 135–136
  overview, 8, 135

Internet browser
  bookmarks, managing, 103, 106
  browsing history, clearing, 114
  browsing history, using, 111–112
  Cloud-accelerated advantages,
      17, 101
  downloading content, 113
  form data, remembering/clearing, 115
  Home screen, accessing from, 101
  Internet searching, 109–111
  libraries, opening from, 35
  location services, enabling/
      clearing, 115
  navigation aids, 101
  overview, 101
  photo viewing/saving options, 113
  predictive pre-loading, 17
  privacy, 18, 107, 114–116
  Reading View, using, 103–104
  search engines, choosing,
      110–111
  searching pages, 108–109
  settings, clearing, 116
  settings, overview, 106–108
  shortcuts panel, 104–105
  tabs, managing, 102
  website data, clearing, 116
investment app, 233–234

● **K** ●

keyboard (onscreen)
  opening, 139, 172, 185
  settings, 54, 71–72
Kindle e-mail account, 121–122
Kindle Fire HDX. *See also* new features
  buttons, location of, 24–25
  computer, connecting to, 46–47
  content, removing, 38
  e-mail account, 121–122, 200
  e-reader capabilities, 125
  gorilla glass, use of, 19
  hardware specifications, 9–10
  headphone/speaker setup, 158
  interface, overview, 32–34

Kindle Fire HDX *(continued)*
  Lending Library access, 17
  locking/unlocking, 26
  music, setting up for, 158
  new features, overview, 7–8
  in-plane switching technology, 19
  power on/off, 26
  protecting, 19
  registrations, 29–31
  setup procedure, 29–30
  sharing options, 189
  storage options, 10
  unpacking, 24
  videos, maximized for, 167
  viewing angle, 175
Kindle FreeTime
  Favorites area, accessing from, 39
  overview, 8
  parental controls, 58
Kindle Matchbook
  overview, 8
  purchasing options, 127
Kindle reading app (computer), 128

• *L* •

Left Nav button
  book navigation, 134
  borrowing books, 127
  Contacts app, 187
  download management, 113
  magazine navigation, 148
  Music library, settings, 155
  Music library, shopping options, 153
  playlists, creating, 162–163
  playlists, editing, 165–166
  Silk browser, navigating in, 103–105,
    111–112
  Videos store, using with, 169, 173
lending library
  accessing, 17, 126
  using, 127–128
libraries. *See also* device libraries
  content, accessing through, 34–38
  Favorites area, adding items to, 40
  finding/accessing, 34–35
  Lending Library, 17, 126–8
  locating/opening books, 132–133
  Overdrive system, 129

  public, borrowing from, 126, 129
  searching in, 45
Location-Based Services
  Parental Controls, settings in, 60
  toggling in Settings, 67
lyrics
  displaying, 160–162
  IMDb database, accessing, 16

• *M* •

magazines
  Amazon, accessing through, 126
  Newsstand, downloading with, 87–90
  purchasing/reading, 148–149
Mahjong app, 252
malware issues, 126
Manage All Applications screen, 67–68
Matchbook
  overview, 8
  purchasing options, 127
Mayday button
  accessing/using, 44
  overview, 7
  transmissions, controlling, 53–54
memory management
  app management, 68, 80
  cache, clearing, 114
  Cloud storage considerations, 10–11, 36
  device reset, 64
  video quality settings, 173
  videos, streaming versus downloading,
    35, 166–168
Miracast devices, flinging to, 177
monitor/TV mirroring, 70
mono/stereo conversion, 73
Monsters Ate My Condo app, 240–241
movies
  flinging, 13, 177
  renting versus buying, 96–97
music
  albums, opening, 158
  Amazon Music Importer, installing/
    using, 156
  Carousel, accessing from, 38
  Cloud, accessing from, 31
  Cloud, archiving in, 36
  computer, transferring content from, 46
  device versus Cloud libraries, 36

Dolby Digital Plus, 151
downloading, overview, 92
Favorites area, accessing from, 39
headphone/speaker setup, 158
Kindle Fire HDX advantages, 151
lyrics, displaying, 160–162
Music library, accessing, 94
Music library, organizing in, 37
Music store library depth, 151
Music store previews, 93
opening/playing songs, 158
player pre-installed, 12
playlists, creating, 162–165
playlists, editing, 165–166
searching library/Cloud/web,
    154–155
sideloading, 151
transferring from computers, 155
uploading to Amazon Cloud, 155–157
X-Ray, using with, 159–162
Music Importer, 156
Music library
  accessing music, 94
  Cloud storage, accessing, 157
  collections, organizing via Cloud, 152
  navigating, 153
  organizing music, 37, 152
  searching, 154
  settings, 155
Music store
  Purchasing content, 93–94
  searching, 155
  song previews, 93
  song titles, availability of, 151

• *N* •

Navigation panel, 46
new Kindle features
  Amazon Assist (Mayday), 23, 53–54
  Amazon Coins, 83–84
  Calendar app, 197, 211–213
  camera improvements, 197
  Cloud Collection, 152
  Cloud Collection feature, 152
  GameCircle, 239
  Matchbook, 8, 127
  Mayday support, 7, 44, 53–54
  Navigation panel, 46

New Oxford American Dictionary, 197,
    221–222
  OfficeSuite Pro, 197
  overview, 7–8
  Quickswitch, 38
  Reading View, 17, 103
  Second Screen, 177
  Silk shortcuts panel, 104, 107
  wireless printing, 197, 207–208
Newsstand app
  Magazine library, accessing,
    126, 147
  managing content, 148
  option bar use, 45–46
  periodicals, browsing/purchasing, 16,
    87–90, 148
note-taking app, 230–231
Notification Sounds setting, 69
notifications
  Alarm Clock app, 228
  Calendar app, 213
  controlling, 8, 53–54, 69
  settings, 69
  Status bar clues, 41–42
  swipe gesture, displaying with, 27

• *O* •

OfficeSuite app
  document, opening, 209
  Dropbox, accessing files from, 209
  editing options, 209–211
  notes/highlighting, 150
  pre-installed functionality, 12
  printing options, 207–208
  SkyDrive, accessing files from, 209
1-Tap-Archive, 8
onscreen keyboard settings, 71
Options bar
  context-sensitive help, 45–46
  e-books, navigating with, 133
  locating, 44–45
  music, using with, 159
Oragami cover, 29
Overdrive, 129
Oxford Dictionary of English
  books, accessing definitions from, 221
  opening with Books button, 221
  searching/locating, 222

• *P* •

pages, turning, 28
Parental Controls
  blocking/unblocking, 59
  Free-Time, 58
  location-based services, 60
  password setup, 59
  Wi-Fi access control, 60
passwords
  clearing, 114
  purchases/content control, 59
  remembering, 114
  screen unlocking, 73–74
  setup screen, 59
  Wi-Fi access control, 60
periodicals
  Amazon, accessing through, 126
  Newsstand, downloading with, 87–90
  purchasing/reading, 148–149
persistent connection, 17
photos
  album organization, 216, 221
  Cloud Drive, managing in, 221
  Contacts app, adding to, 185–186
  deleting, 221
  downloading methods, 216
  editing options, 218–220
  email, receiving pictures, 31
  file formats supported, 203
  sharing methods, 48, 217
  social networks, sharing through, 189–191
  taking with Camera app, 214–215
  viewing options, 217
  viewing/editing, 12
  viewing/saving options, 113–114
Photos app
  contact records, adding pictures to, 185–186
  editing options, 218–220
  overview, 213
  sharing pictures from, 48, 190
  sideloading pictures, 199–200
  viewing options, 217
playlists
  creating, 162–165
  editing, 165–166

power saving (sleep), 70
pre-installed apps
  Amazon Shopping, 97–98
  Calendar, 197, 211–213
  Camera, 214–215
  Contacts, 181
  dictionary, 143
  listing, 12, 225
  OfficeSuite, 209–211
  overview, 12
  Photos, 213
Prime (Amazon)
  membership advantages, 19–21, 128, 167
  membership cost, 169
  Prime Instant Video access, 167
  streaming video access, 20
Prime Instant Video, 167, 169
printing
  options, 207–208
  overview, 8
  SketchBook Mobile images, 226
privacy
  Internet browser, 18, 107, 114–116
  Reset to Factory Defaults, 64–65
  Silk browser, 18
productivity tools, 197
progress bar, 135

• *Q* •

Quell Memento app, 243–244
Quick Settings. *See also* Settings button
  Airplane Mode, 52
  Amazon Assist (Mayday), 53–54
  Auto-Rotate, 50–51
  Brightness, 51
  Mayday button, accessing/using, 44
  opening, 43, 49–50
  Quiet Time, 8, 53, 69
Quick Switch
  apps, opening with, 38
  overview, 8
Quiet Time
  controlling/scheduling, 69
  overview, 8
  toggling, 53

• *R* •

reading app (computer), 128
Reading View, 103–104
resetting factory defaults, 64–66

• *S* •

screen
   brightness controls, 51, 70
   orientation control, 50–51
Screen Magnifier, 73
Screen Reader, 71
search engines
   browser history, using, 111–112
   choosing, 110–111
   internet searching, 109–110
Search in Book option, 140
Search the Web option, 140
Search Wikipedia option, 140
Second Screen
   flinging movies, 177
   overview, 8
security
   Amazon malware protection, 126
   privacy, 18, 64–65, 107, 114–116
   settings, 73
serial number, displaying, 64
settings
   Airplane Mode, toggling, 52
   Auto-Rotate, 50–51
   Brightness, 51
   full menu, accessing, 43
   keyboard, 54, 71–72
   Mayday transmissions, 53–54
   overview, 49
   Quick Settings, opening, 49–50
   Quick Settings, using, 43
   Quiet Time, toggling, 53
Settings button
   Contact Us option, 57–58
   Device settings, 61–66
   Help, 57–58
   My Account, 55–57
   overview, 54–55
   Parental Controls, 58–61
   Sync All Content, 55

User Guide, 57
   wireless connection troubleshooting, 57
Share features
   photo sharing options, 48
   social networks, using with, 134, 146,
      189–191
   websites, using with, 114
Shop Amazon app, 97–98
sideloading
   Cloud storage/backup, 200
   definition, 13
   docs from computer, 199–200
   overview, 13, 38
   photos, 216, 226
   USB cable, using for, 46–47
Silk browser
   bookmarks, managing, 103, 106
   browsing history, clearing, 114
   browsing history, using, 111–112
   Cloud-accelerated advantages, 17, 101
   content filtering/prediction, 17
   downloading content, 113
   form data, remembering/clearing, 115
   Home screen, accessing from, 101
   Internet searching, 109–111
   libraries, opening from, 35
   location services, enabling/clearing, 115
   navigation aids, 101
   overview, 101
   photos, downloading, 216
   photos, viewing/saving options, 113
   predictive pre-loading, 17
   privacy, 18, 107, 114–116
   Reading View, using, 103–104
   search engines, choosing, 110–111
   searching pages, 108–109
   settings, clearing, 116
   settings, overview, 106–108
   shortcuts panel, 104–105
   tabs, managing, 102
   website data, clearing, 116
SketchBook Mobile, 226–227
SkyDrive, 209
Skype app
   Contacts, using with, 193
   credits, obtaining/using, 194
   downloading, 191

Skype app *(continued)*
multiple messages, sending, 194
profile, editing, 194
Settings, accessing, 194–195
setup, 192–193
testing, 192
video calls, making, 13
video/voice calls, making, 193
sleep function, 70
social networks
accounts, setting up, 30
apps, downloading, 189
photos, downloading, 216
photos, sharing options, 48
sharing content from Kindle, 189–191
Solitaire Free Pack app, 249–250
songs
lyrics, displaying, 160–162
Music store previews, 93
opening/playing, 158
playlists, creating, 162–165
playlists, editing, 165–166
searching library/Cloud/web, 154–155
X-Ray, using with, 159–162
sound
keypress settings, 71
Notification Sound previews, 69
Quiet Time, controlling with, 53
volume control, 69–70
spell-checking, 71
spreadsheets, 11–12, 209
status bar, overview, 41–43
stereo/mono conversion, 73
stock market app, 233–234
storage
Cloud options, 12–13, 221
device specifications, 9
device versus Cloud, 10–11, 36
Stray Souls: Dollhouse Story app, 245
streaming
definition, 35
downloading versus, 167–168
videos, 20, 35
swipe gestures. *See also* gestures
accessibility tools, 72
Appstore navigation, 80

page turning, 133
Quick Settings, using, 43
Quick Switch, using, 38
scrolling, 169
touchscreen, using with, 27–29
Sync All Content, 55
system updates, 62

• *T* •

tablets
definition, 7
Kindle Fire advantages, 7
text enlarging, 28
Text-to-Speech
reading e-books, 145
voice choices, 62
Time & Date settings, 62–63
Today's Free App of the Day, 80
touchscreen, 27–29
TV/monitor mirroring, 70
Twitter
accounts, setting up, 30
app download, 189
photo sharing options, 48
pre-installed functionality, 12
sharing content from Kindle, 189–191

• *U* •

USB cable, connecting for data transfer, 46–47
User Guide
Accessibility Tools, 73
Help topics, 57

• *V* •

videos
downloading/removing, 170
Kindle Fire HDX, maximized for, 167
opening/playing, 173–177
overview, 95
playback tools, 175–176
player pre-installed, 12

Prime Instant Video, 167
quality preference, setting, 173
recording with Camera app, 216
renting versus buying, 96–97
resuming, 174–175
samples, viewing, 96
streaming access, 20
streaming versus downloading,
    35, 167–168
Whispersync, resuming with, 170
Videos store
accessing/opening, 170
categories, shopping by, 169–171
filtering, 173
IMDb database, accessing, 176
navigating categories, 170–171
searching, 172
Videos button access, 167–168
Watchlist, creating, 172
X-Ray, using with, 176

• W •

Watchlist
Add to Watchlist button, 97
creating in Videos Store, 172
weather app, 231–233
Where's My Perry? app, 242–243
Whispersync
audiobooks, syncing, 126
downloading apps, 14
Immersion Reading, 15
managing storage with, 36

overview, 126
syncing with, 14
videos, resuming with, 170
Wi-Fi
access control, 66
connection options, 99–100
Wifi Analyzer, 236–237
wireless connections
setup options, 66–67
troubleshooting, 57
word processing
ColorNote Notepad Notes,
    230–231
OfficeSuite app, 207–211
Words with Friends Free app, 251
Wordsmith app, 248–249

• X •

X-Ray
displaying information, 179
music, using with, 159–162
overview, 8, 125, 178
using with books, 137–138
videos, using with, 176, 178

• Z •

Zip files, 203
zooming gestures
fixed layout constraints, 135
pinching/unpinching, 28

About the Author

Nancy Muir is the author of more than 100 books on technology and business topics. In addition to her writing work, Nancy has written a regular column on computers and the Internet on Retirenet.com and is Senior Editor for the website UnderstandingNano.com. Prior to her writing career, Nancy was a manager at several publishing companies and a training manager at Symantec.

Dedication

To Megan, Laurie, and Debi, the ladies at Blue Heron Jewelry in Poulsbo who keep me motivated to write books.

Author's Acknowledgments

With this book I got to work with Susan Christophersen, who was assigned to lead the team on this book as well as perform the copy editing. Susan, you kept up with a ridiculous schedule admirably and I hope we work together often. Thanks also to Earl Boysen for his able work as technical editor. Last but never least, thanks to Katie Mohr, my favorite Acquisitions Editor, for giving me the opportunity to write this book.

Publisher's Acknowledgments

Senior Acquisitions Editor: Katie Mohr

Project and Copy Editor: Susan Christophersen

Technical Editor: Earl Boysen

Editorial Assistant: Annie Sullivan

Sr. Editorial Assistant: Cherie Case

Project Coordinator: Patrick Redmond

Cover Images: Background ©iStockphoto.com/ VikaSuh; Hardware and screenshot courtesy of Nancy Muir; Back cover images courtesy of Nancy Muir

Mac

Dummies,
n
-49823-1

For Dummies,
n
-35201-4

For Dummies,
n
-20920-2

ntain Lion
mies
-39418-2

& Social Media

For Dummies,
n
-09562-1

gging
mies
-03843-7

For Dummies
-32800-2

ss For Dummies,
n
-38318-6

ities For Dummies,
on
-01687-9

For Dummies,
on
0-90545-6

Personal Finance
For Dummies,
7th Edition
978-1-118-11785-9

QuickBooks 2013
For Dummies
978-1-118-35641-8

Small Business Marketing Kit
For Dummies,
3rd Edition
978-1-118-31183-7

Careers

Job Interviews
For Dummies,
4th Edition
978-1-118-11290-8

Job Searching with
Social Media
For Dummies
978-0-470-93072-4

Personal Branding
For Dummies
978-1-118-11792-7

Resumes For Dummies,
6th Edition
978-0-470-87361-8

Success as a Mediator
For Dummies
978-1-118-07862-4

Diet & Nutrition

Belly Fat Diet For Dummies
978-1-118-34585-6

Eating Clean For Dummies
978-1-118-00013-7

Nutrition For Dummies,
5th Edition
978-0-470-93231-5

Digital Photography

Digital Photography
For Dummies,
7th Edition
978-1-118-09203-3

Digital SLR Cameras &
Photography For Dummies,
4th Edition
978-1-118-14489-3

Photoshop Elements 11
For Dummies
978-1-118-40821-6

Gardening

Herb Gardening
For Dummies,
2nd Edition
978-0-470-61778-6

Vegetable Gardening
For Dummies,
2nd Edition
978-0-470-49870-5

Health

Anti-Inflammation Diet
For Dummies
978-1-118-02381-5

Diabetes For Dummies,
3rd Edition
978-0-470-27086-8

Living Paleo For Dummies
978-1-118-29405-5

Hobbies

Beekeeping
For Dummies
978-0-470-43065-1

eBay For Dummies,
7th Edition
978-1-118-09806-6

Raising Chickens
For Dummies
978-0-470-46544-8

Wine For Dummies,
5th Edition
978-1-118-28872-6

Writing Young Adult Fiction
For Dummies
978-0-470-94954-2

Language & Foreign Language

500 Spanish Verbs
For Dummies
978-1-118-02382-2

English Grammar
For Dummies,
2nd Edition
978-0-470-54664-2

French All-in One
For Dummies
978-1-118-22815-9

German Essentials
For Dummies
978-1-118-18422-6

Italian For Dummies
2nd Edition
978-1-118-00465-4

Available in print and e-book formats.

wherever books are sold. For more information or to order direct: U.S. customers visit www.Dummies.com or call 1-877-762-2974.
customers visit www.Wileyeurope.com or call (0) 1243 843291. Canadian customers visit www.Wiley.ca or call 1-800-567-4797.

Connect with us online at www.facebook.com/fordummies or @fordummies

Math & Science

Algebra I For Dummies,
2nd Edition
978-0-470-55964-2

Anatomy and Physiology
For Dummies,
2nd Edition
978-0-470-92326-9

Astronomy For Dummies,
3rd Edition
978-1-118-37697-3

Biology For Dummies,
2nd Edition
978-0-470-59875-7

Chemistry For Dummies,
2nd Edition
978-1-1180-0730-3

Pre-Algebra Essentials
For Dummies
978-0-470-61838-7

Microsoft Office

Excel 2013 For Dummies
978-1-118-51012-4

Office 2013 All-in-One
For Dummies
978-1-118-51636-2

PowerPoint 2013
For Dummies
978-1-118-50253-2

Word 2013 For Dummies
978-1-118-49123-2

Music

Blues Harmonica
For Dummies
978-1-118-25269-7

Guitar For Dummies,
3rd Edition
978-1-118-11554-1

iPod & iTunes
For Dummies,
10th Edition
978-1-118-50864-0

Programming

Android Application
Development For
Dummies, 2nd Edition
978-1-118-38710-8

iOS 6 Application
Development For Dummies
978-1-118-50880-0

Java For Dummies,
5th Edition
978-0-470-37173-2

Religion & Inspiration

The Bible For Dummies
978-0-7645-5296-0

Buddhism For Dummies,
2nd Edition
978-1-118-02379-2

Catholicism For Dummies,
2nd Edition
978-1-118-07778-8

Self-Help & Relationships

Bipolar Disorder
For Dummies,
2nd Edition
978-1-118-33882-7

Meditation For Dummies,
3rd Edition
978-1-118-29144-3

Seniors

Computers For Seniors
For Dummies,
3rd Edition
978-1-118-11553-4

iPad For Seniors
For Dummies,
5th Edition
978-1-118-49708-1

Social Security
For Dummies
978-1-118-20573-0

Smartphones & Tablets

Android Phones
For Dummies
978-1-118-16952-0

Kindle Fire HD
For Dummies
978-1-118-42223-6

NOOK HD For Dummies,
Portable Edition
978-1-118-39498-4

Surface For Dummies
978-1-118-49634-3

Test Prep

ACT For Dummies
5th Edition
978-1-118-01259-8

ASVAB For Dumm
3rd Edition
978-0-470-63760-

GRE For Dummies
7th Edition
978-0-470-88921-

Officer Candidate
For Dummies
978-0-470-59876-

Physician's Assist
For Dummies
978-1-118-11556-5

Series 7 Exam
For Dummies
978-0-470-09932-

Windows 8

Windows 8 For Du
978-1-118-13461-0

Windows 8 For Du
Book + DVD Bund
978-1-118-27167-4

Windows 8 All-in-
For Dummies
978-1-118-11920-4

 Available in print and e-book formats.

Available wherever books are sold. For more information or to order direct: U.S. customers visit www.Dummies.com or call 1-877
U.K. customers visit www.Wileyeurope.com or call (0) 1243 843291. Canadian customers visit www.Wiley.ca or call 1-800-567
Connect with us online at www.facebook.com/fordummies or @fordummies